THE ENGLISH LANDSCAPE GARDEN

*Examples of the important literature
of the English landscape garden movement
together with some earlier garden books*

Edited with introductory notes by

JOHN DIXON HUNT

A GARLAND SERIES

THE SEATS
OF THE NOBILITY AND GENTRY

In a Collection of the most interesting
and Picturesque Views

William Watts

Garland Publishing, Inc.
New York • London
1982

For a complete list of the titles in this series
see the final pages of this volume.

This facsimile has been made from a copy in
the Lewis Walpole Collection of the Yale University Library.

Library of Congress Cataloging in Publication Data

Watts, William, 1752–1851.
   The seats of the nobility and gentry in a collection
of the most interesting and picturesque views.

   (The English landscape garden)
   Reprint. Originally published: Chelsea, London :
W. Watts, 1779.
   1. Historic buildings—England.   2. England—History,
Local.   I. Title.   II. Series.
DA660.W33   1982   942   79-56982
ISBN 0-8240-0169-9   AACR2

Design by Jonathan Billing

The volumes in this series are printed on acid-free,
250-year-life paper.

Printed in the United States of America

PREFACE

William Watts (?1752–1851) received his training from Paul Sandby and Edward Rooker. After engraving and publishing this collection he travelled abroad.

The Seats of the Nobility and Gentry is a fine gathering of views of country seats and surrounding parklands that proclaim variously the vogue for "Capability" Brown's landscapes of smooth, sweeping lawns interspersed with clumps of trees and the picturesque taste for more "busy" and seemingly wilder terrain. The views are engraved from drawings by Sandby, Thomas Hearne, and others and are accompanied by notes on locations and owners (these last often rather excessive in their flattery). There is very little duplication of scenes in this and the similar volume by Angus (see The Seats of the Nobility and Gentry in Great Britain and Wales, also reprinted in this series). Both works are handsome examples of an increasingly popular genre of publication—popular with owners, who liked to see their property displayed, and tourists alike. Such works are also an essential source for landscape history, for which see John Harris, A Country House Index, Pinhorns, Isle of Wight, 1971.

J.D.H.

The SEATS of the Nobility and Gentry,

In a Collection of the most interesting & Picturesque VIEWS,

Engraved by W. WATTS

From Drawings by the most eminent Artists.

With descriptions of each VIEW.

Published by W. Watts, Kemp's Row, Chelsea – January 1st 1779.

R. Shepherd Sculp.

An ALPHABETICAL INDEX of the Names or Titles of POSSESSORS of SEATS contained in this Work.

A.   Plate

Afhburnham, Earl of, - - - LXI
Aftley, Sir Edward, - - XXXVIII
Afgill, Sir Charles, - - - - XXXV
Afhton, Nicholas, Efq. - LXXVI

B.

Bute, Earl of, - - - - - - - LXV
Ditto, - - - - - - - - - - - LXIX
Ditto, - - - - - - - - - - LXXIII
Bulkeley, Vifcount, - - - - - XL
Baffett, Sir Francis, - - - XXXIV
Broadhead, T. H. Efq. - - - LX
Byng, George, Efq. - - XXVIII

C.

Clive, Lord, - - - - - - - - VI
Clavering, Sir Thomas, - LXXVII
Conftable, William, Efq. - - XII
Coke, William, Efq. - - - XXXIX
Conyers, John, Efq. - - - XXVII
Child, Mrs. - - - - - - - - LXX

D.

Devonfhire, Duke of, - - - XXX
Ditto, - - - - - - - - - - - L
Ditto, - - - - - - - - - - LXXXI
Dick, Sir John, - - - - - LXII
Kaye, John Hatfield, Efq. - - XX
Drummond, Robert, Efq. - XXIV

E.   Plate

Exeter, Earl of, - - - - - XXI
Ditto, - - - - - - - - - - XLI
Egmont, Earl of, - - - - - LIV
Ellis, Welbore, Efq. - - XLVIII
Elvil, Sir John, - - - - - LXVI

F.

Fortefcue, Lord, - - - LXXIV

G.

Gower, Earl, - - - - - - XXXI
Griffin, Sir John Griffin, - XXVI
Garrick, Mrs. - - - - - LXVIII

H.

Holroyd, John Baker, Efq. - III
Heron, Thomas, Efq. - - LXXII
Hallett, William, Efq. - - - XL

K.

Kaye, John-Hatfield, Efq. - - XX
Knight, Thomas, Efq. - - LXVII

L.

Lothian, Marchionefs of, - - - I
Legh, Peter, Efq. - - - - LXXIX
Legh, Henry Cornwall, Efq. LXIV
Lafcelles, Edwin, Efq. - - - VII

M.   Plate

Milford, Lord, - - - - - - - II
Milton, Lord, - - - - - XXXIII
Methuen, Paul, Efq. - - XXXII
Meadows, Philip, Efq. - - - XVI

N.

Northumberland, Duke of, XLIX
Ditto, - - - - - - - - - - LVII
Norfolk, Duke of, - - - - XIII
Newcaftle, Duke of, - - - XXIX

O.

Orford, Earl of, - - - - - XLVI
Ofborn, Sir George, - - - - XXV

P.

Percy, Earl, - - - - - - - LVIII
Pembroke, Earl of, - - - LXXXII
Petre, Lord, - - - - - - - XVII
Petre, J. Berney, Efq. - - XLIV
Prefton, Jacob, Efq. - - - XXXVI
Portman, W. H. Efq. - LXXXIII

Q.

Queenfbury, Duke of, - - - - IX

R.

Rockingham, Marquis of, - - V
Romney, Lord, - - - - - - LV
Ryves, Thomas, Efq. - - - VIII

S.   Plate

Suffolk, Earl of, - - - - - XLV
Scarborough, Earl of, - - - - X
Salifbury, Earl of, - - - - LIII
Strathmore, Earl of, - - - XLII
Strafford, Earl of, - - - - - LI
Scarfdale, Lord, - - - - - XXII
Stanley, Sir William, - - XXIII
Smyth, Sir William, - - - XVIII
Smith, Mrs. - - - - - - - LXXV
Smyth, John, Efq. - - - LXXXIV
Sawbridge, John, Efq. LXXVIII
Sawrey, J. Gilpin, Efq. - LXXX

T.

Tylney, Earl of, - - - - - - LVI
Torrington, Vifcount, - - XXXVII
Townfhend, Vifcount, - - - LII
Tynte, Sir Charles, - - - - - XV
Turner, Greg. Page, Efq. XLVII
Trecothick, James, Efq. - - XIX

V.

Vanneck, Sir Gerard, - - XLIII

W.

Walpole, Lord, - - - - - - LIX
Waltham, Lord, - - - - - - IV
Worfley, Sir Richard, - - - XIV
Weld, Humphrey, Efq. - - LXXI
Walker, Ifaac, Efq. - - - LXIII

ERRATA.

Defcription I. Line 9, for Vincinity, read Vicinity.

       III. For J. B. Holroyd, Efq. read Right Honourable Lord Sheffield.

       XXI. Line 5, for refem, read refembling.

       XXIV. Line 5, for is, read are.

       XXV. Line 3, for his, read the.

       XXVI. For Sir John Griffin Griffin, read Right Honourable Lord Howard.

P. Sandby r.a. del. W. Watts sculp.

West Combe, *in Kent, the* Seat *of the Marchioneſs of* Lothian.

Publiſh'd as the Act directs Jan.ᵗ 1.ˢᵗ 1779, by W. Watts, Kemp's Row, Chelsea.

PLATE I.

WEST COMBE,

NEAR GREENWICH, IN KENT,

The Seat of the Marchionefs of LOTHIAN.

Drawn by P. SANDBY Efq. R. A.

A N agreeable Eminence, from which many picturefque Views are continually commanded, renders this Seat peculiarly happy in its Situation. The Building, though not magnificent, may boaft of Elegance. In the midft of a thick and venerable Grove it rifes to the Eye with an Air of *propreté*, more eafily imagined than defcribed. The Pleafure-Grounds around are laid out with fo much Tafte, as to render them a perfect Scene of rural Simplicity. The Variety of floating Objects beheld (from the Front of the Houfe) upon the *Thames* at a confiderable Diftance off (and thofe, from its ferpentine Courfe, rendered much more brilliant and enlivening) muft neceffarily claim our Attention, efpecially if we include a Multitude of Cattle continually grazing on each Side of the River's verdant Banks. *Lime-Houfe* Church affords us a *Coup d' Oeil*, and a Bird's-Eye Landfcape of *London*, with the Adjacent Hills of *Highgate* and *Hampftead* in the Back-Ground there terminates the View.

Notwithftanding the Vincinity of this Seat to the Metropolis, yet from the Advantage of *Greenwich* Park on the Left, *Charlton* on the Right, and *Blackheath* to complete the Whole, we may, without Hefitation, pronounce it one of the moft defirable Spots in *England*.

C. Hendley R.A. del.

W. Watts sculp.

Picton Castle *in Pembrokeshire, the* Seat *of* Lord Milford .

Publish'd as the Act directs, Jan.y 1.st 1773. by W. Watts, Kemp's Row, Chelsea.

PLATE II.

PICTON CASTLE,

IN PEMBROKESHIRE.

The Seat of the Right Honourable Lord MILFORD.

Drawn by P. SANDBY, Esq. R. A.

From a Sketch by the Hon. CHARLES GREVILLE.

PICTON CASTLE, *Pembrokeshire,* is situate about three Miles from *Haverford-Weſt,* and nine from *Milford-Haven,* (one of the moſt ſecure and commodious Harbours in *Great-Britain.)* The Antiquity of the Edifice may be partly aſcertained by conſulting the Records ſo far back as in the Reign of *William Rufus, Anno* 1087, at which Time *William de Picton,* a *Norman* Knight, who came into the Country with *Arnulph* of *Montgomery,* who laid the Foundation of *Pembroke-Caſtle,* and was afterwards created Earl of *Pembroke,* took Poſſeſſion thereof. Thro' defect of Iſſue Male, it deſcended from them to the *Wogans,* then to the *Donnes,* and laſtly to the much eſteemed and well known Family of the *Phillips* of *Kylſant,* in whoſe Poſſeſſion it has continued for eight Generations, and is now the Reſidence of the Right Honourable Lord *Milford,* who has modernized the Ground, by a pleaſing Plantation of Firs and Evergreens. There is a noble Park, well ſtocked with Deer. From the upper Part of the Caſtle you command, in a clear Day, a beautiful and extenſive View of *Milford-Haven.* Of all the Caſtles in *Wales* this is the only one which remains entire, the others being in Part, if not totally, deſtroyed. That its Antiquity or Service might not be buried in Oblivion, it is here to be remarked, that it received additional Luſtre from having ſuſtained (during the Time of that unhappy Monarch *Charles* the Firſt) a long Siege in defence of his Majeſty, under the Command of that intrepid General Sir *Richard Phillips.*

Sheffield Place *in Sussex, the Seat of* John Baker Holroyd *Esq.*

Published as the Act directs, Jan.y 1.st 1779, by W. Watts, Kemp's Row, Chelsea.

PLATE III.

SHEFFIELD PLACE,

IN SUSSEX.

The Seat of JOHN BAKER HOLROYD, Efq.

Drawn by P. SANDBY Efq. R. A.

THE Houfe is very large, and pleafantly fituated in a beautiful and extenfive Park, midway between *Eaft Grinftead* and *Lewes*. The firft Foundation is not known; but it has undergone fuch great Alterations, efpecially within a few Years, that the ancient Building can fcarcely be traced. It has lately been much enlarged; a confiderable Part rebuilt; and the whole ornamented with great Propriety and Tafte, at a large Expence by the prefent Poffeffor. The Outfide is in the beft Gothic Tafte, enriched with Pinnacles, and a beautiful Chapel Window, the whole being light, chearful and elegant. In a Gothic Frize, which goes round the Houfe, are introduced the Arms of the Poffeffors of the Lordfhips of *Sheffield* from the Conqueft to this Time, viz. of *De Morton* or *Mortaigne*, half Brother to the Conqueror, of *Lancafter, Norfolk, Dorfet, Abergavenny, Delawar*, &c. Within is a fine fuite of Apartments, fome very fingular. A magnificent Staircafe is an Example of the Beauty and Elegance of the Gothic Style, when the Parts are well chofen and properly employed. The fcenery, in general, is uncommonly pleafing, to which the clufter Columns and painted Glafs contribute very much. There are feveral good Pictures in the Apartments, and a Ceiling, which for Elegance of Defign and good Painting, is not furpaffed. The diftant and near Views from the Houfe are extremely fine; the Entrance into the Park is through a large Gothic Arch, fhaded by great Trees. On each Side are Apartments for the Gate-Keeper. The Garden Grounds contain upwards of one hundred Acres. Thefe and the Park have every Advantage of Water, Diverfity of Ground, large Timber, and fine Shrubs, with feveral fingularly fine Views of the fouth Downs and neighbouring Country.

James Littell del.   W. Watts sculp.

New Hall *in* *Essex,* the Seat of Lord Waltham.

Published as the Act directs, Jan.y.1.1779. by W. Watts, Kemps Row, Chelsea.

PLATE IV.

NEW HALL,

IN ESSEX,

The Seat of the Right Honourable Lord WALTHAM.

Drawn by the Honourable JAMES LUTTRELL.

NEW HALL, fo called to diftinguifh it from the Manor of *Old Hall*, is fituate about two Miles N. E. of *Chelmsford*, and has been inhabited by fome of the firft Perfonages of this Kingdom. In 1450 it was in the Poffeffion of the *Ormond* Family ; and in 1524 became the Refidence of *Henry* VIII. who, with all royal Magnificence and Splendor, here celebrated the Feaft of St. *George*. The Lady *Mary*, his Daughter, afterwards Queen of *England*, lived here fome Years, as did alfo Queen *Elizabeth*, who paffed a Grant of thefe Premifes to *Thomas Ratcliff*, Earl of *Suffex*, together with all the Honors, elegant Buildings, extenfive Park, and Demefnes thereunto belonging. After this it centered in the Duke of *Buckingham*'s Family, till purchafed in 1651 by *Oliver Cromwell*. Soon after the glorious Reftoration, it reverted to the *Buckinghams*, and was then bought of them by General *Monk*, afterwards Duke of *Albemarle*. In 1737 this venerable and noble Palace became the Property of the late Lord *Waltham*, Baron of *Philips-Town* in the Kingdom of *Ireland*, during whofe Life it underwent many and material Alterations. The great Gate-way, towards the South, together with the Eaft and Weft Sides, were pulled down. The much-admired Painted-Window, now in St. *Margaret*'s Church, *Weftminfter*, formerly ornamented the Chapel belonging to this fumptuous Structure. That Part of the Edifice which remains at prefent, was then the North and South of two capacious Quadrangles, and now contains not only many State-Rooms, but alfo one of the nobleft Halls in the Kingdom, being ninety-fix Feet in Length, upwards of forty high, and fifty broad, from one Bow-Window to the other. In this Hall, over the Door defcribed in the Plate, are the Arms of King *Henry* VIII. fo elaborately cut and finifhed, in Free-Stone, that we may, without Hefitation, pronounce them to be the *Chef d'Oeuvre* of the Artift. Defcription falls fhort of the Sculptor's Merit ; the niceft ocular Examination can only do him Juftice. From the following Infcription, cut in old Characters,

Henricus Rex Octavus, Rex inclitus Armis
Magnanimus, ftruxit hoc Opus egregium,

we are led to conclude the *front* Court, at leaft, was built by his Majefty, efpecially as thefe Arms were formerly placed over the great Gateway, though now affixed, for their better Prefervation, in this noble Room, the Ceiling of which is richly ornamented with Stucco-Work ; in the Center are his Lordfhip's Arms ; at each End his Creft : two other Parts are adorned with Cherubims, who are reprefented on the Wing, but in the Attitude of fupporting Chains of Chandeliers. Over the South Door (fronting a fpacious Avenue, which confifts of four Rows of lofty Limes, the Tops of which carefs each other) are feen the Arms of Queen *Elizabeth*, moft chaftly executed in Stone, with the following complimentary Italian Diftich :

En Terra la piu favia Regina, en Cielo la piu lucenta Stella

Vergine magnanima Dotta, divina, ledgiadra, honefta et bella.

The prefent Right Honourable and worthy Poffeffor, to do juftice to fo noble a Piece of Architecture, has, at a very great Expence, accompanied with true Tafte, laid out the Grounds thereunto belonging in fo judicious and pleafing a Manner, as to perpetuate the diftinguifhed Appellation given to that Situation, in the Height of its Glory, viz. *Beaulieu.*

P.Sandby del.   _W.Watts sculp.t_

Wentworth House, _in Yorkshire, the Seat of the Marquis of_ Rockingham.

Publish'd as the Act directs April 1.st 1779, by W.Watts, Hemp's Row, Chelsea.

PLATE V.

WENTWORTH HOUSE,

In *YORKSHIRE.*

The Seat of The MARQUIS of ROCKINGHAM.

(Drawn by THOMAS SANDBY, Esq. Professor of Architecture to the Royal Academy.)

WENTWORTH House is pleasantly situated between *Rotherham* and *Barnsley*, in one of the most delightful Parks in *England.* The Building is equalled by few in Magnificence, the principal Front being six hundred Feet in Length, including two extensive Wings. In the Center is a noble Portico, sixty Feet by twenty in the area, supported by eight *Corinthian* Columns, three Feet in Diameter, to which we are led by two grand Flights of Steps, adorned with Balluftrades. The Pediment is enriched with the Arms of the Family, and the Top of the Building with a Range of light Statues ; between are Vases, which are continued round the Center upon a handsome Balluftrade.

The rustic Floor consists of a very large Arcade, and two Suites of Rooms. In the Arcade is a fine Group, in Statuary, of three Figures, as large as Life, by *Foggini.* Upon the principal Floor we first enter the grand Hall, which is sixty Feet square and forty high ; round it is a Gallery ten Feet wide, supported by eighteen fluted Ionic Columns, in Imitation of Marble, admirably executed ; between the Columns are Niches for Statues, and over them excellent Basso Relievos in Pannels, from Designs by Mr. *Stewart.* Above the Gallery are eighteen Pilasters of the Corinthian Order, which are likewise in Imitation of Marble ; between are Pannels, in Stucco, over which from the Capitals, are Festoons of the same : the whole in a Style which cannot fail of exciting Admiration.

From the Hall we are conducted through two magnificent Suites of Apartments furnished in the most elegant Manner ; the Library is sixty Feet by twenty, and the Gallery a hundred and thirty Feet by eighteen ; the Ceilings are enriched with Ornaments in Stucco ; and the Chimney-pieces exquisitely carved. These Apartments contain some fine Pictures, among which is an excellent Copy from *Vandyke* of *Henrietta* Queen of *Charles* I. by Lady *Fitzwilliams* ; the Earl of *Strafford* and his Secretary by *Vandyke* ; *Diana* and *Endymion*, and *Cymon* and *Iphigenia*, by Mr. *West* ; with several other good Performances.

The

The Park which furrounds the Manfion is very extenfive, and moft beautifully diverfified with magnificent Woods, Hills, and large Vallies, through which a Sheet of Water two hundred Yards in Width, ferpentines in the moft agreeable Manner, on the Margin of which is an octagon Temple, and over it an handfome Bridge.   The Gardens have their proper Enrichments of Pavilions, Grottos, Statues, Urns, &c.   Among feveral fine Buildings the pyramidal Tower deferves particular Attention; it is two hundred Feet in Height, and built on the Summit of a very high Hill, at a Diftance from the Houfe; the Afcent is by a winding Stair-cafe, and from the Top is the moft aftonifhing and delightful Profpect that can be conceived.   The Building with all its furrounding Hills, Groves, Lawns, Waters, &c. break at once upon the Eye, and around them an amazing Tract of cultivated Inclofures.   Over the Entrance is the following Infcription :

MDCCXLVIII.

" This pyramidal Building was erected by his Majefty's moft dutiful Subject, *Thomas* Marquis of *Rockingham*, &c. in grateful refpect to the Preferver of our Religion, Laws and Liberties, King *George* the Second, who, by the Blefling of God, having fubdued a moft unnatural Rebellion in Britain, Anno 1746, maintains the Balance of Power, and fettles a juft and honourable Peace in *Europe*."

There is likewife an Aviary, built in the *Chinefe* Manner, well ftocked with foreign Birds, which are kept alive in the Winter by means of hot Walls at the Back of the Building; the Front is open Net-work in Compartments.   Alfo a Menagerie, a noble Ionic Temple, and feveral other curious and beautiful Structures, too numerous to particularize in this Undertaking.

G. Barrett R.A. pinxt.   W. Watts Sculp.

Claremont, *in Surry, the Seat of* Lord Clive.

Published as the Act directs April 1.st 1779, by W. Watts, Kemp's Row, Chelsea.

PLATE VI.

CLAREMONT,

A Villa, belonging to the Right Honourable Lord CLIVE;

Situated in *SURRY*, about *Fifteen Miles* from *LONDON*.

(Painted by *GEORGE BARRETT, Efq. R. A.*)

THIS Villa has received from Nature and Art fuch liberal Advantages as have brought it the neareft to Perfection of any in this Kingdom; and is certainly an Inftance where great Expence has produced Grandeur, Convenience, Firmnefs, Delight, and Enjoyment. It has rifen gradually to this Perfection. A Publication in 1731 [*Campbell's Britannicus*] fpeaks highly of the Gardens, Plantations and Profpect from the Tower, the Top of which is juft feen over the Trees in this Plate. His Grace the Duke of *Newcaftle*, the then Proprietor, employed moft liberally Sir *John Vanburgh* and *Kent*, the greateft Artifts of their Time, and this gave to the Situation all that was wanted towards a large and excellent Kitchen-Garden, fpacious Offices for Stabling, Farm, Brewing, Wafhing, &c. an excellent Aqueduct, by which the whole Eftablifhment is amply fupplied with good Water. The Park and Gardens were planted and decorated with lively and emblematical Buildings, and confiderable Additions were made to the Houfe; but this being ill fituated, thefe Additions were calculated to ferve only the prefent Turn, and it was left for the next Proprietor, the late Lord *Clive*, to build a new Houfe in a more eligible Situation, and to make fuch Alterations in the Plantations and Approach as fhould give to the Grounds that delightful and elegant Characteriftic which is fo peculiar to the Works of the modern Artift. To bring this about, the Bufinefs could not have fallen into better Hands. The noble Proprietor had Ambition, great Ideas, Confidence, Difcernment, and a great Fortune; accordingly he directed the Houfe to be built, which is fo happily defigned and fituated, as to command fine Views from the four Fronts. It contains large, numerous, and well-finifhed ftate and private Apartments. The Approach is grand, and convenient to the Portico, for Company; it is concealed and convenient for the Tradefmen and Servants, to the Offices; and the Gardens may boaft a very fuperior and finifhed Elegance.

M. A. Rooker pinx.^t   W. Watts sculp.^t

Harewood House, in Yorkshire, the Seat of Edwin Lascelles Esqr

Published as the Act directs, April 1.st 1779, by W. Watts, Kemp's Row, Chelsea.

PLATE VII.

HAREWOOD HOUSE,

In *YORKSHIRE.*

The Seat of EDWIN LASCELLES, Efq.

(Painted by M. A. ROOKER.)

THIS noble Manſion, ſituate in the Weſt Riding of *Yorkſhire*, is about eight Miles from *Harrowgate Spa*, and in the direct Road from thence to *Leeds*; it is very large, extending in Front two hundred and fifty Feet, and for Grandeur of Style in the Compoſition, and Elegance of decorating and finiſhing both externally and internally, deſervedly ranked with the firſt Buildings in this Kingdom. The Wings of the North Front are enriched with emblematical Medallions, executed in a maſterly Manner, by *Collins* from the Deſigns of *Zucchi*; in the Center is a handſome Pediment ſupported by ſix Three Quarter Corinthian Columns, thirty Feet in Height, which compoſe the Entrance from a Flight of Steps to a noble Hall of the *Doric* Order, decorated with Statues, Urns, &c. from whence we are conducted through a Range of Apartments, furniſhed in the moſt magnificent Manner. The South Front (ſeen in the Plate) has a noble Portico of four Columns, from whence the Eye paſſing over an extenſive Slope, is led to a ſpacious Sheet of Water, gently wind- ing in a Serpentine Courſe, beyond which the Country forms one of the moſt beautiful Scenes imaginable; and to the North, over a fertile Vale, interſected by the River *Wharfe*, is ſeen *Alms Cliff*; this vaſt Rock, which riſes with prodigious Grandeur, is viſible at forty Miles diſtance.

Near this Seat are the Remains of *Harewood Caſtle*, a Place of great Antiquity. There is alſo a ſmall Church, containing many an- cient Monuments, among which is that famous one of Lord Chief Juſtice *Gaſcoyne*, who had the Reſolution to commit Prince Henry, (afterwards Henry V.) to the King's Bench, for ſtriking him at Weſtminſter, while he was in the Seat of Juſtice; for which Act of Regard to the Authority of the King, more than to the Image of his Perſon, the Prince himſelf, when he came to the Throne, not only forgave, but juſtified him.

Mr.

Mr. *Lafcelles*, the prefent Poffeffor of the above defcribed Seat, has politely fixed every Saturday as a public viewing Day for his Houfe and Grounds, of which Permiffion the Nobility and Gentry who frequent *Harrowgate*, avail themfelves much, the flight Diftance therefrom being a moft agreable Excurfion.

It may not be amifs to obferve, that *Alms Cliff* is fuppofed to derive its Name from the Diftribution of Alms there at certain ftated Times, agreeable to the Tenor of Legacies left to the Chapel which originally ftood there, and was at that Time dedicated to the *Virgin Mary*.

We are indebted to Meffrs. *Adams* and Mr. *Carr*, of *York*, for the Defign of this fine Piece of Architecture; and for the prefent beautiful Difpofition of the Pleafure-grounds, Gardens, Waters, &c. to Mr. *Brown*, of *Hambton-Court*.

S. Hearne del.   W. Watts sculp.

Ranston, *in Dorsetshire, the Seat of* Thos *Ryves Esqr*

Published as the Act directs, April 1.st 1779, by W. Watts, Kemp's Row, Chelsea.

PLATE VIII.

RANSTON,

In *DORSETSHIRE,*

The Seat of THOMAS RYVES, Esq. F. R. S.

(*Drawn by T. HEARNE.*)

THIS beautiful Seat has received great Alterations and Improvements from the prefent Poffeffor, who, in the Year 1758, defigned and built the Front, feen in the Plate annexed, containing a fpacious Saloon and Drawing-Room. The old Part of the Edifice appears to have been erected about the Time of King *Henry* the VIIIth, but the ancient and modern Parts are united with fuch Propriety, and correfpond fo well, that the whole appears uniform ; and, we may fay with Truth, that few Houfes of its Dimenfions contain fo many elegant Apartments. This Manfion has been in the Poffeffion of the prefent Family near two Centuries—It is pleafantly fituated in a fine Vale, about four Miles from *Blandford* and eight from *Shaftfbury*—The Profpect from the Houfe is much enriched by *Hod* and *Hamilton* Hills, which lie near and have a very picturefque Appearance ; on the firft of which is to be feen the moft perfect Encampment now remaining of the *Danes* or *Romans,* but generally fuppofed to be the Work of the former—at the Foot of this Hill runs the River *Stour* ; its Acclivity renders it almoft inacceffible, and from the Top is feen the whole of *Blackmoor's* rich luxuriant Vale. On *Hamilton* Hill are two remarkable Eminences, called by the Peafants *Giants' Graves,* fuppofed to have been the burial Places of thoufands flain in Battle at thofe Times, tho' Hiftory does not particularize this Circumftance ; neither has Mr. *Hutchins,* in his Account of *Dorfetfhire,* paid fufficient Attention to thefe remarkable Places.

There has been here formerly a large Village and Chapel, but at prefent there only remains two fmall Cottages befides this Manor-Houfe, tho' there are in a Field adjoining, called *Chapel-Hays,* Traces of many Buildings, and the Root of a large Yew, fuppofed to be near where the Chapel ftood.

P. Sandby. R.A. delin.t   W. Watts sculp.t

The Duke of Queensbury's Palace, at Drumlanrig in Scotland.

Published as the Act directs, August 1.st 1779, by W. Watts, Kemp's Row, Chelsea.

PLATE IX.

THE
DUKE of QUEENSBERRY's PALACE,

At DRUMLANRIG in SCOTLAND.

(Drawn by P. SANDBY, Esq. R. A.)

WILLIAM Duke of *Queensberry* is said to have began this noble Edifice in 1679, and to have compleated the same in 1689 : it stands on the Side of an immense Hill, embosomed by lofty Trees : at each Angle of the Court within the Building is a round Tower, and in every one a Staircase leading to numerous Apartments : the Gallery is a hundred and eight Feet long, contains many good Portraits by various Masters, and is very richly ornamented with carved Work finely executed by *Gibbons*.

In the Park, which is well wooded and watered, we meet with the white Breed of wild Cattle, peculiar to this Part of the Country for many Ages back ; they are more shy than any Deer, and so remarkably timorous as to set off full gallop on the least Noise or even Appearance of a human Being : they are of a middle Size, with long Legs ; the Orbits of their Eyes, and the Tips of their Noses are Black ; the Cows are finely horned, but the Bulls have lost the Manes attributed to them by *Boethius*.

Drumlanrig, which gives the Title of Earl to the Dukedom, is not indebted to the most elevated Parts of the Grounds for its only Beauties, for the Walks by the Side of the *Nith*, which runs at the Bottom of a deep and wooded Glen, affords us Scenes most picturesque and various, improved also by the View of an handsome Bridge of two Arches, rising high above the River : from the Summit we behold a Depth which strikes the Soul with Horror, and that much increased by the rapid and foaming Torrents (coloured with a deep moory Tint) variously divided by broken and sharp-pointed Rocks.

Here is a fine Road, between twenty and thirty Miles in length ; and the Woollen Manufactory of Stuffs and Stockings, which gives Bread to thousands, thereby increasing Population, has been kept in heart by the several Premiums thrown out by the late Duke for the Encouragement thereof : an Example worthy imitation.

W. Hodges pinx.^t   W. Watts sculp.^t

Sand-beck, *in Yorkshire, the* Seat *of the* Earl *of* Scarborough.

Published as the Act directs, Augt 1.st 1779, by W. Watts, Kemp's Row, Chelsea.

PLATE X.

SANDBECK,

In YORKSHIRE.

The Seat of The Earl of SCARBOROUGH.

(Painted by WILLIAM HODGES.)

FROM the peculiar Elegance of this noble Edifice and its delightful Situation, we need not hefitate in pronouncing it to be in every refpect, one of the moft complete and defirable Places in this Kingdom. It has been brought to this Degree of Perfection by the prefent Earl (a Nobleman diftinguifhed by his fine Tafte in the polite Arts) under the Direction of *James Paine*, Efq. from whofe Defigns it was erected. The whole Building is of an excellent Free-ftone from *Roch Abbey*, which is about a Mile diftant: the Capitals and other ornamental Parts well executed, and the Pediment of the Portico decorated with a fine Alto Relievo, by the ingenious Mr. *William Collins*. It contains many handfome and convenient Apartments, well adapted to their refpective Purpofes.

The principal Floor confifts chiefly of a Drawing-Room, Hall, two Dining-Rooms, and a fpacious Saloon, which opens at the Eaft End into a magnificent Portico, of the *Compofite* Order, commanding a moft agreeable Profpect of the adjacent Country. The Chapel, Stables, &c. which are large Buildings, are entirely fcreened from the Houfe by a fine Wood.

Sandbeck is fituated in the Weft Riding of the County of *York*, near the Confines of *Nottinghamfhire*, on a moft fertile Soil, furrounded by extenfive Woods, fine Hills and rich Vallies, diverfified by a large Piece of Water: the natural Beauties of this Place probably induced his Lordfhip to improve and ornament it, it having been confidered only as a Villa; *Lumley-Caftle*, in the County of *Durham*, being the ancient Seat of this noble Family.

C. Metz pinx.t   W. Watts sculp.t

Baron-Hill, *in the Isle of Anglesey, the Seat of Lord Viscount* Bulkeley.

Published as the Act directs, August 1.st 1779, by W. Watts, Kemp's Row, Chelsea.

PLATE XI.

BARON-HILL,

In the Isle of ANGLESEY.

The Seat of The Right Hon. Lord Viscount BULKELEY.

(Painted by C. METZ.)

BARON-HILL, the Seat of Lord *Bulkeley*, is agreeably situated on an Eminence, richly wooded, on the east Part of the Island, commanding a beautiful and extensive View of the Town and Castle of *Beaumaris*, the Sea, and River *Menai*, terminating with the immense Range of the Mountains of *Caernarvonshire*, at the Foot of which runs the great *Irish* Post-road to *Holyhead*. It has been the Residence of this Family from the Time of Queen *Elizabeth*, but has lately received such material Alterations and Improvements by the present noble Possessor, under the Direction of Mr. *Samuel Wyatt*, that it may almost be said to have been rebuilt.

The House consists of a spacious Dining-Room, two Anti-Rooms, a Drawing-Room and Breakfast-Parlour to the South East; a Library to the North East, and a Hall to the North West. The Grounds, which are very beautiful, have been laid out and improved under the Direction of Mr. *Emes*.

J. Barret R. A. pinxt.

W. Watts sculpt.

Burton Conſtable, in Yorkſhire, the Seat of Wm Conſtable Eſq.

Publiſh'd as the Act directs Augt 5t 1779, by Mr Watts, Kemp's Row, Chelsea.

PLATE XII.

BURTON CONSTABLE,

In *HOLDERNESS in the County of YORK.*

The Seat of WILLIAM CONSTABLE, Esq.

(Painted by GEORGE BARRET, Esq. R. A.)

BURTON CONSTABLE was built about the reign of *Henry* VIII. The north Tower and Wing, if family Tradition may be credited, were built as early as the Reign of King *Stephen* ; an Opinion, however, which most probably is erroneous ; as it is agreed by almost all the learned in Antiquity, that no large Brick Buildings were erected in *Britain* before the Time of *Henry* VIII. were very scarce during that Reign, and even not in common Use till the latter End of Queen *Elizabeth.*

Great Improvements and material Alterations have been made within the last twenty Years.

The Stables, Gardens, Menagerie, and one Wing of the House, lately built.

The Grounds, Park, Piece of Water, and Bridge, were laid out and executed under the Direction of *Lancelot Browne,* Esq.

The Situation rather flat, but well wooded. Some gentle Risings in the Park have a pleasing Effect.

The Stables were built and the Alterations of the House were chiefly made from Designs of the late Mr. *Lightholder.*

The Dimensions of some of the principal Rooms are as follow :

		L.	B.	H.
Great Hall	——	60 Feet.	30 Feet.	30 Feet.
Staircase	—	45	30	30
Drawing Room	—	45	30	20
Eating Parlour	——	36	24	16
Gallery	—	110	20	16

A well-

A well-chosen Library of about ten Thousand Volumes.

A good Collection of Paintings; some Originals of the best Masters.

A large valuable Collection of old MSS. including those of the late Dr. *Burton* of *York*, F. A. S. Author of the *Monasticon Eboracense*. The second Vol. of this esteemed Work is in MS. in this Collection. These MSS. would be of the greatest Assistance towards Compiling the natural and civil History of this large, opulent, and important County.

Some Statues and Basso Relievos, executed by that able and ingenious Artist Mr. *Collins* of *London*.

A curious equatorial Instrument by the late Mr. *Hindley* of *York*; whose great and untaught Abilities were well known, and often instructive to some of the greatest Astronomers and Mathematicians of this Age.

Three Views of *Burton Constable* by Mr. *Barret*.

T. Malton delin.   W. Watts sculp.

Workſop Manour Houſe, in Nottinghamſhire, the Seat of the Duke of Norfolk.

Published as the Act directs Jan. 1st 1780, by W. Watts, Kemp's Row, Chelsea.

PLATE XIII.

WORKSOP MANOUR-HOUSE,

In *NOTTINGHAMSHIRE*,

The Seat of the Duke of NORFOLK,

(*Drawn by THOMAS MALTON, Jun.*)

WORKSOP MANOUR-HOUSE is fituated upon an agreeable Rife, in the Center of an extenfive Park, weftward of *Workfop* in *Nottinghamfhire*, a Market Town, at the Head of the River *Ryton*, famous for its Abbey, which was founded by *William de Lovetoft*, in the Year 1103. The Structure is of Stone, and though upwards of 300 Feet in extent, is but an inconfiderable Part of a moft magnificent Palace, which the late Duke of *Norfolk* had directed to be built on this Spot, and of which his Grace (attended by the Duchefs, the Hon. Mr. *Edward Howard*, Heir apparent, with feveral of the neighbouring Gentry) laid the Foundation-ftone on the 25th of *March*, 1763; and continued to carry on the Work with fuch Spirit, that the whole of the prefent Range of Building was completely finifhed in 1765, but the Death of Mr. *Howard*, which unfortunately happened the following Year, put a Period to the completion of this Defign, which is the more particularly to be regretted, as this Palace, if it had been finifhed agreeable to the Intention of the noble Founder, would doubtlefs have been unequalled by any in the Kingdom.*

This Edifice is erected upon the fame Spot the ancient Manfion ftood, which was built by the Countefs of *Shrewfbury*, in the Reign of Queen *Elizabeth*, and was for fome Time the Refidence of the noble Family of *Talbot*: it had received feveral Alterations and Improvements from the different Poffeffors till the Year 1759, when the Duke of *Norfolk* came to a Refolution of new modelling and fitting up the various Apartments, and for this Purpofe had, in the Courfe of two Years, expended upwards of 22,000*l*. the Alterations were nearly completed, when, unhappily, on the 22d of *October*, 1761, the whole Building was burnt to the Ground, together with a large and valuable Library, a curious Collection of Pictures by the moft celebrated Mafters, a vaft Quantity of fuperb Furniture, &c. The Lofs by this dreadful Accident was eftimated at 100,000*l*. It lay in Ruins for about eighteen Months, but the Spirit of the Duke furmounted all Difficulties, and in a fhort Time, the prefent elegant Fabrick rofe, like a Phœnix, from its Afhes.

* The Defigns for the different Fronts, &c. of this Seat will be given in the fecond Volume of the Works of *James Paine*, Efq. which will fpeedily be publifhed.

A. Devis del.   W. Watts sculp.

Appuldurcombe Park, in the Isle of Wight, the Seat of Sir Richard Worsley Bart.

Published as the Act directs, Jan 7th 1780, by W Watts, Kemp's Row, Chelsea.

PLATE XIV.

APPULDURCOMBE PARK,

In the ISLE of WIGHT,

The Seat of the Right Honourable Sir RICHARD WORSLEY, Bart.

(Drawn by A. DEVIS.)

THE Houſe is pleaſantly ſituated in the Park, about ſeven Miles South of the Town of *Newport:* it has four regular Fronts of the *Corinthian* Order, built with Freeſtone ; the Pilaſters, Cornices, and other ornamental Parts, of Portland. The Principal Entrance is through a Hall of fifty-ſix Feet by twenty-four, divided by *Scaliogli* Columns of the *Ionic* Order, in imitation of Porphyry : this and the other Apartments on the ground Floor are enriched with many valuable Portraits and other good Paintings.

The Houſe was begun by the late Sir *Robert Worſley* in the Year 1710, but left in a very unfiniſhed State :. it is now completed by Sir *Richard Worſley*, who has made conſiderable Additions and much improved upon the original Deſign.

The Entrance into the Park, which is well ſtocked with Deer, is through a handſome Gateway of the *Ionic* Order : the Soil is very rich and affords excellent Paſturage : the Eminences command moſt extenſive and grand Proſpects : on the Eaſt is ſeen *St. Helen's* Road, *Spithead* and *Portſmouth* ; on the Weſt, *Freſhwater* Cliffs, the *Dorcheſter* Coaſt, and the Iſle of *Portland* ; on the North, is a View of the New-Foreſt, and the Channel, by which the Iſland is ſeparated from the other Part of the County ; and on the South is the *Britiſh* Channel : from hence alſo, the Iſland itſelf, with all its variety of beautiful Scenery, appears to the greateſt advantage.

Appuldurcombe was formerly a Monaſtery of the *Benedictine* Order, held under the Abbey of *Lyra*, in *Normandy*, and ſuppreſſed in the ſecond Year of *Henry* V. *Anno Dom.* 1414. It was afterwards granted to the Abbeſs and Nuns of the *Minories*, of the Order of St. *Clare*, without *Aldgate* ; and at the Diſſolution of Monaſteries, in the Time of *Henry* VIII. ſold to Sir *James Worſley*, Knight, then Captain of the *Iſle* of *Wight*, and Dame *Anne*, his Wife, and their Heirs in Fee Farm.

Halfwell, *in Somersetshire, the Seat of Sir Charles Kemeys Tynte, Bar.*

Publish'd as the Act directs, Jan 1.st 1780, by W. Watts, Kemp's Row, Chelsea.

PLATE XV.

H A L S W E L L,

In SOMERSETSHIRE,

The Seat of Sir CHARLES KEMEYS TYNTE, Bart.

(Painted by J. RICHARDS, Esq. R. A.)

HALSWELL, the Seat of Sir *Charles Kemeys Tynte*, is pleasantly situated about four Miles South-West of *Bridgewater*, in the County of *Somerset :* it has been the Residence of this Family many Years, and was rebuilt in 1689.

Nature has happily dressed this Spot with pure Water, good Timber, rich Verdure, and fertile Hills ; and it commands the *Bristol* Channel to make the Scene completely picturesque.

J. Barret R.A. del.   W. Watts sculp.

The Lodge, in Richmond-Park, the residence of Philip Medows Esq.

Publish'd as the Act directs, Jan.1.1780, by W. Watts, Kimps Row, Chelsea.

PLATE XVI.

The LODGE in RICHMOND PARK,

The Residence of PHILIP MEDOWS, Esq.

(Drawn by GEORGE BARRET, Esq. R. A.)

THE House was originally a Deer-keeper's Lodge, but the late Sir *Robert Walpole*, when Ranger of this Park, was so well pleased with the Situation, that he resided here frequently, having built two handsome Wings, containing some good Apartments, and made such other Improvements for that Purpose, as rendered it a most desirable Retreat. It commands a fine View over an extensive Lawn, terminated on each Side by Groves of Oak ; and in Front, at about a Third of a Mile distance, are two fine Pieces of Water, beyond which are rising Woods. Behind the Building, to the South-East, the Ground rises to a considerable Height, and from this Eminence, which is crowned with lofty Elms and Clumps of Beech, you have the most delightful inland Prospect. The Park is of very great Extent, containing 2250 Acres, and is well planted with Oak and other Timber, some of which, however, is rather in the Decline. In this Park his present Majesty, about sixteen Years since, made a noble Plantation of Forest Trees, near four Miles in length ; which, as they have already grown in a surprising Manner, may probably turn out of great Utility.

J.Watts del.t et Sculp.t

Thorndon Hall *in Essex, the* Seat *of* **Lord Petre.**

Published as the Act directs, May 1st 1780, by W. Watts, Kemp's Row, Chelsea.

PLATE XVII.

THORNDON HALL,

IN ESSEX,

The Seat of the Right Honourable Lord PETRE.

THORNDON HALL was erected by the prefent noble Poffeffor in the Year 1770, from the Defigns of *James Paine*, Efq. and may with the greateft Propriety, be ranked in the firft Clafs of Buildings which adorn this Country. It is moft happily fituated on a rifing Ground, in a fine Park, about two Miles South-eaft of *Brentwood* in *Effex*, commanding the moft delightful Profpects of the adjacent Country. The Park and Grounds had been much improved with various and extenfive Plantations, by the late Lord, and a confiderable Progrefs made in refitting and modernizing the ancient Seat (which was built by Sir *William Petre*, in the Year 1591, and was fituated about two Miles South of the prefent Edifice) but his Lordfhip's Death prevented the further Profecution of this Plan. The prefent Nobleman, then a Minor, happily attaining his Age, gave Orders for pulling down the old Structure, and rebuilding it on the prefent eligible Spot: it was accordingly began and carried on with great Rapidity and Succefs, Permiffion having been given for drawing unlimitted Sums to facilitate the Undertaking, a Circumftance probably unprecedented: and indeed the whole both of the external and internal Workmanfhip claims Admiration, and fufficiently evinces that neither Expence or Labour has been fpared in order to render it compleat, and worthy of the Refidence of its illuftrious and opulent Founder.

The Dimenfions of the principal Apartments of *Thorndon Hall*:

Hall	40 Feet in Length	40 Feet in Width and	32 in Height.
Saloon	60	30	32
Drawing Room	45	25	27
Little Drawing Room	36	22	18
Dining Room	36	24	18
Library	95	20	18
Chapel	48	24	32

Plans, Elevations and Sections of this Building will be given in Mr. *Paine*'s Publication.

T. Sandby delt.   W. Watts sculpt.

Hill Hall, *in Essex, the* Seat *of* Sir Wm. Smyth Bar.t

Published as the Act directs, May 1st 1780, by W. Watts, King's Row, Chelsea.

PLATE XVIII.

HILL HALL,

In ESSEX,

The Seat of Sir WILLIAM SMYTH, Bart.

(Drawn by THOMAS SANDBY, Esq.)

THE Manſion-houſe at *Hill Hall* in *Eſſex* was built in the Year 1568 by Sir *Thomas Smyth*, Knight, Secretary of State in the Reigns of King *Edward* VI. and Queen *Elizabeth*.

The South and Eaſt Fronts are here repreſented ; the Length of each is about 140 Feet.

Within the Court, the original Stile of Architecture made Uſe of in this Structure, may be obſerved greatly reſembling that of So-merſet-Houſe, (the late Building): It is probable that Sir *Thomas* employed the ſame Architect as his Patron, the Protector Duke of *Somerſet* ; we are told his Name was *John* of *Padua*. *Longleat* in *Wiltſhire*, the Seat of Lord *Weymouth*, and other magnificent Build-ings were erected in the ſame Taſte, which at that Period was newly introduced from *Italy*.

The grand Suite of Apartments forming one Side of the Court, was deſigned with Symmetry of Proportion and Elegance, the Rooms are ſpacious and lofty, commanding beautiful and extenſive Proſpects. The Hall is 54 Feet long, 30 broad, and 25 in Height.

The principal Front was much improved and altered in the Year 1714, by Sir *William Smyth*, Grandfather of the preſent Baronet.

.J. Carter del.

J. W. Watts sculp.

Addington Place, *in* Surry, *the Seat of* James Ivers Trecothick *Esq.*

Published as the Act directs, May 1st 1780, by W. Watts, Kemp's Row, Chelsea.

PLATE XIX.

ADDINGTON-PLACE,

In SURREY.

The Seat of JAMES IVERS TRECOTHICK, Efq.

(Drawn by J. CARTER.)

THE Houfe is pleafantly fituated upon an agreeable Eminence, near the Village of *Addington*, about three Miles South Eaft of *Croydon* in *Surrey*, and commands a moft beautiful Profpect of an extenfive and romantic Country: It was erected from the Defigns, and under the Direction of *Robert Mylne*, Efq. The whole is of Portland Stone, exceeding neat, and well executed, and the Apartments are large, convenient, and well proportioned.

I. Malton delt.   _W. Watts sculp._

Hatfield Hall _in Yorkshire, the_ Seat _of_ John Hatfield Kaye _Esqr._

Publish'd as the Act directs May 1st 1780. by W. Watts, Kemp's Row, Chelsea.

PLATE XX.

HATFIELD HALL,

In YORKSHIRE.

The Seat of JOHN HATFIELD KAYE, Efq. F.S.A.

(Drawn by T. MALTON, Junior.)

THIS Place was formerly called *Woodhall,* and has a Manor appertaining thereto, as appears by an Inquifition in the Chapel of the Rolls, Anno 21 Hen. VII. It was in the year 1608 rebuilt by *Gervafe Haitfield,* Efq. Defcendant of Sir *Stephen Haytfeeld,* Knight, High Sheriff for the County of *Gloucefter,* 3 Hen. VI. who was of a branch of an ancient Family of that Name, refident at *Hatfield* in *Holdernefs,* in the *Eaft Riding* of *Yorkfhire.* In 1715 it grew into Decay, the whole being much defaced and contracted by *Ofwald,* Great Grandfon to the former Poffeffor, till the Year 1768, when the prefent Proprietor enlarged, ornamented, and greatly improved the whole.

    Hatfield Hall is delightfully feated at the Head of a rich Vale, near *Wakefield* in *Yorkfhire,* in a luxuriant Country, and commands the moft beautiful Profpects, to which the noble Seats of the Earls of *Huntingdon* and *Mexborough,* with the River *Calder,* and the Villages of *Kirkthorpe* and *Heath,* are no inconfiderable addition. The Building has three different Fronts in the *Gothic* ftyle, and contains feveral handfome and convenient Apartments, neatly finifhed in the fame tafte.

A. Davis del.

W. Watts sculp.

Burghley House, in Northamptonshire, the Seat of the Earl of Exeter.

Published as the Act directs Sep.r 1.st 1780, by W. Watts, Kemp's Row, Chelsea.

PLATE XXI.

BURGHLEY HOUSE,

IN NORTHAMPTONSHIRE,

The Seat of the Right Honourable the Earl of EXETER.

(Drawn by A. DEVIS.)

WILLIAM CECIL, Lord *Burghley*, Lord High Treasurer to Queen *Elizabeth* (the Ancestor of the present Earl) erected this spacious and noble Edifice, since which it has been at different Times much improved. It stands on the Borders of *Northamptonshire*, on a rising Ground, and commands an extensive Prospect for near thirty Miles, over *Stamford*, into the Fens of *Lincolnshire*. The House is quadrangular, built all of Free-Stone, and has, from its Magnitude, and the Number of Towers and Pinnacles it is adorned with, at a little distance, the appearance of a Town, to which it has been frequently compared, the large Spire over the Clock in the Center, resembling the principal Church.

At this Seat the celebrated *Verrio* spent twelve Years; he had a Table, an Equipage, and a considerable Pension allowed him, in consequence of which, there is a Profusion of excellent Paintings in the different parts of the House; the Stair-Case, the Cielings of several of the State Apartments, the Chapel, the Earl's Closet, and the great Hall, are compleatly decorated with the Performances of this admired Master. There are also several other much esteemed Pictures at *Burghley*, and one in particular of the Death of *Seneca*, by *Luca Jordano*, for which, it is said, six thousand Pistoles was offered by *Lewis* the fourteenth.

Great Alterations and Improvements have been made in the Disposition of the Grounds and Water, particularly in the Approach to the House, under the Direction of *Lancelot Brown*, Esq. of *Hampton Court*, by the present Noble Possessor.

G. Barret R.A. delt.   W. Watts sculp.

Kedleston House *in Derbyshire,* **the Seat** *of* **Lord Scarsdale.**

Published as the Act directs, Sep.r 2.d 1780, by W. Watts, Kemps Row, Chelsea.

PLATE XXII.

KEDLESTON HOUSE,

IN DERBYSHIRE,

The Seat of the Right Honourable Lord SCARSDALE,

(Drawn by G. BARRET, Efq. R. A.)

KEDLESTON HOUSE, we may venture to affert (if not unequalled) is inferior to none in this Kingdom, in any refpect ; the ftyle of Architecture is uncommonly beautiful, and worthy of Admiration : the proportion of the Wings, as well as of the Portico, to the Center, are judicioufly obferved, and produce a pleafing Effect. The Portico confifts of fix Corinthian Columns with their correfponding Pilafters, three Feet in Diameter, which fupport a handfome Pediment, decorated with light Statues. The Center is united to the Wings by Corridors, which project in an agreeable fweep, forming together one magnificent Front, three hundred and fixty Feet in Extent. The Entrance to the principal Story, is by a double Flight of Steps, which lead through the Portico to a noble Hall, fixty-nine Feet by forty two, adorned with eighteen Columns of Alabafter, of the Corinthian Order, twenty-five Feet in height, the Entablature richly ornamented ; nothing can furpafs this Room in Elegance : between the Columns are fine antique Statues in Niches, over which are Baffo Relievos in Compartments, crowned with Feftoons ; the Ceiling is arched, and highly finifhed in Stucco ; in the Center is a large Window, by which the whole receives Light ; the height to the Top of this Window is forty feven Feet. The Saloon to which the Hall communicates is a circular Room, forty-two Feet in Diameter, and fifty five in height, terminating in a Dome ; the Ceiling finifhed in Mofaic Work ; it contains fome good Statues, and Baffo Relievos, and is light in the fame Manner as the Hall, by a Window from the Summit. The Dimenfions of the other principal Apartments, are as follow :

Drawing Room	44	by	28 Feet
Dining Room	36	—	24
Mufic Room	36	—	24
Library -	36	—	24

Thefe Rooms are finifhed in the moft fuperbtafte, and embellifhed with feveral valuable Paintings, by *Raphael, Guido, N. Poufin, Rembrandt, Annibal Carracci, Claude Lorraine,* and other Eminent Mafters.

Kedlefton is fituated upon a gentle Rife, in the Center of a fine Park, about four Miles from *Derby,* and commands from every Part the moft delightful Profpects. The Pleafure-Grounds are laid out with great Tafte, in a ftyle anfwerable to the Magnificence of the Building, and the Park abounds with noble Plantations of Oak and other Timber agreeably interfperfed.

This Building was erected from the Defigns of *Robert Adam,* Efq.

D. Dalby del.

W. Watts sculp.

Hooton *in Cheshire, the* Seat of *Sir* Wm *Stanley Bar.*^t

Published as the Act directs, Sepr 2, 1780, by W. Watts, Kemp's Row, Chelsea.

PLATE XXIII.

HOOTON,

IN CHESHIRE,

The Seat of Sir WILLIAM STANLEY, Bart.

(Drawn by Mr. D. DALBY.)

THE prefent Structure was erected in the Year 1778, from a Defign of Mr. *Samuel Wyatt*'s upon the fame Spot the ancient Building ftood, which was for feveral Ages the refidence of the *Stanleys*.

The Houfe is large, elegant and commodious, and the interior Ornaments finifhed in a very fine Tafte: it is built of Stone, procured from a Quarry at *Storeton*, belonging to Sir *William*, which merits particular Notice, being fuperior in Colour to *Portland*, and of an excellent Quality. Very few Villas can boaft of a Situation comparable to *Hooton*: the Profpect is diverfified with Hills, Woods and Water. At the Foot of an eafy Slope, at the diftance of about half a Mile, runs the River *Merfey*, and all Veffels trading from *Liverpool*, to *Warrington*, *Manchefter*, and the Duke of *Bridgewater*'s Canal, pafs in full View from the Houfe, which likewife commands the continuation of the River below *Liverpool*, with the Town and Shipping in the Harbour, which lies about eight Miles Northward: the principal Towers and Spires of *Chefter*, are feen about the fame diftance to the South, and have the appearance of rifing out of a very extenfive intervening Wood, beyond which *Beefton Caftle*, likewife erects its Head. The Lawn in Front of the Houfe is bounded by a fine Wood, from the Skirts of which there is an extenfive View of the *Welch* Hills which overlook the Vale of *Clywd*.

Poole Hall, which is feen in the Diftance, in the annexed Plate, is an antient Seat of the *Pooles*, and at prefent belongs to Sir *Ferdinand Poole*, Bart.

G.t Barret R.A. del.

W. Watts sculp.

Cadland Park, *in Hampshire, the Seat of* **Rob.t Drummond** *Esq.r*

Published as the Act directs, Sep.r 5.t 1780, by W. Watts, Kemp's Row, Chelsea.

PLATE XXiv.

CADLAND PARK,

IN HAMPSHIRE,

The Seat of ROBERT DRUMMOND, Efq.

(Drawn by G. BARRET, Efq. R. A.)

THIS Edifice is pleafantly fituated on the Banks of the *Southampton* River, and commands fine Profpects of *Spithead*, the *Ifle* of *Wight*, and a richly wooded Country, abounding with grand and picturefque Objects: the Town of *Southampton*, *Netley Abbey*, the *South Downs*, *St. Helen*'s, &c. appear to the greateft advantage, and the whole Scene is much enlivened by innummerable Veffels, continually failing paft. The Houfe and Offices are new, not large, but aim at convenience and neatnefs, in which refpect they are generally faid to have fucceeded. The Park Enclofure makes a Circumference of about five Miles, the contents of which have probably from the Creation been wild and uncultivated, but is now bringing into high Perfection, and the Owner has the immediate Satisfaction of feeing this new drefs'd Spot in fuch Beauty, as few others with the aid of long Cultivation, have arrived at; the Soil is rich; Plenty of good Water; vaft Quantities of fine old Timber; with every other Effential, requifite for the Gardens, Pleafure Grounds, &c.

The point of View takes in the Houfe, part of the *Southampton*-River, *Calfhot-Caftle*, and *Spithead*.

Chicksands Priory *in Bedfordshire the Seat of Sir George Osborn Bar.*

Published as the Act directs, Jan 1.st 1781. by W. Watts, Chelsea.

PLATE XXV.

CHICKSANDS PRIORY,

IN BEDFORDSHIRE,

The Seat of Sir GEORGE OSBORN, Bart.

THIS Religious Houſe is preſerved intire in the Form in which it was built in the Year 1307. It was of the *Gilbertine* Order; founded and endowed, by *Peganus* of *Beauchamp*, and the Counteſs *Rohaiſa*, in the Reign of *Edward* II. and granted at the Time of the Diſſolution of the Monaſteries, to Sir *Peter Oſborn*, Treaſurer-Remembrancer of his Exchequer.

The Grounds have been greatly altered and improved by the preſent Poſſeſſor, and afford every where a pleaſing Diverſity of Wood, Water, and Lawn; the Style of Gardening called the *Ferme Ornée* is preſerved with great Chaſtity, and the variety of Seats ſuited to the different Scenes, are ſtriking and beautiful; an Hermitage, a Cathedral Seat, connected to a *Gothic* Ruin of a Chapel dedicated to St. *Mary*, in which is preſerved the Burying-Place of the Monaſtery, with ſeveral other characteriſtic Buildings, are placed with great Taſte and Propriety, and are all pleaſingly adapted to the Antiquity of the Place.

Chickſands is ſituated about a Mile Weſtward of *Shefford*, in *Bedfordſhire*, upon a Branch of the *Ivel*, which runs into the River *Ouſe* before it reaches the Town of *Bedford*.

Audley House *in Essex, the* Seat *of* Sir John Griffin Griffin K.B.

Published as the Act directs, Jany 1.st 1781 by W. Watts, Kemp's Row, Chelsea.

PLATE XXVI.

AUDLEY HOUSE,

IN ESSEX,

The Seat of General Sir JOHN GRIFFIN GRIFFIN, Knight of the Bath.

(Drawn by W. DONN.)

AUDLEY HOUSE, or, as it is more commonly called, *Audley End*, was built by *Thomas Howard*, Earl of *Suffolk*, Lord High Treasurer in the Reign of *James* I. and was so called in honour of his Grandfather *Lord Audley*. It is said, the Earl designed it as a Palace for his Majesty, who objected to it on account of its Magnificence, and replied when it was presented to him, " that it would suit a Lord Treasurer very well, but was too much for a King." It remained therefore, in the Possession of the *Earls* of *Suffolk* during that, and the succeeding Reign, but was afterwards purchased by King *Charles* II. It was then the largest Royal Palace in the Kingdom. The Expence of building it is said to have amounted to ninety thousand Pounds. It consisted of two Courts, one of which, and part of the other, including a Gallery two hundred and twenty six Feet long, thirty two wide, and twenty four high, were taken down about seventy Years ago, by *Henry* Earl of *Suffolk*, (it having been granted back again to that Family soon after the Revolution.) The Part which remains at present, though of considerable Extent, is estimated to be about a fourth only of the original Structure.

AUDLEY HOUSE is situated about a Mile South of *Saffron Walden*, in *Essex*, and commands pleasing and diversified Prospects from the four different Fronts. The River *Cam*, which has the Appearance of a fine Canal, and is adorned with two elegant Bridges, is seen gliding through the Lawn from the West, the East exhibits an extensive Park, with the Church and Town of *Saffron Walden*, the South overlooks the Pleasure Grounds, and the North several Plantations, and a neighbouring Village.

This Place has been greatly improved by the present Owner, Sir *John Griffin Griffin*, whose Ancestor *Edward* first Lord *Griffin*, married Lady *Essex Howard*, the eldest Daughter and Coheir of *James* third Earl of *Suffolk*.

W. Watts del. et sculp.

Copped Hall *in Essex, the Seat of John Conyers Esq.*

Published as the Act directs, Jan 1st 1781, by W. Watts, Chelsea.

PLATE XXVII.

COPPED HALL,

IN ESSEX,

The Seat of JOHN CONYERS, Efq.

COPPED HALL is fituated on an agreeable Eminence, about a Mile to the Left of the Fourteen Mile Stone, on the Road to *Epping*. This Place formerly belonged to the Abbots of *Waltham*, but fince the Diffolution of the Monafteries it paffed into the Family of the *Conyers*---The Father of the prefent Poffeffor, *John Conyers*, Efq. took down the ancient, ruinous, though ftately Edifice, and in the Year 1753, built the prefent elegant Manfion.

W. Watts del.t et sculpsit.

Wrotham Park *in Middlesex,* the Seat *of* George Byng *Esq.*

Published as the Act directs, Jan.y 1.st 1781 by W. Watts, Kemp's Row, Chelsea.

PLATE XXVIII.

WROTHAM PARK,

IN MIDDLESEX,

The Seat of GEORGE BYNG, Efq.

THIS Edifice is fituated on a rifing Ground, near *Mims*, on the Borders of *Middlefex*, in an agreeable though fmall Park, bounded by the *Hatfield* and *St. Alban*'s Roads. It was the Refidence of the late Admiral *Byng*, by whom it was built, from the Defigns of Mr. *Ifaac Ware*, and may be confidered, excepting trifling Inaccuracies, as an excellent Compofition in Architecture. It extends two hundred Feet in Front, and is adorned with a noble Portico of Ionic Columns, three Feet in Diameter. The Entrance is by a double Flight of Steps, which project from the Building, on a Semi-circular Plan, and have a pleafing Effect. The Apartments are convenient, and well proportioned, and command from the elevated Situation of the Houfe, the moft beautiful Profpects of the adjacent Country.

The Elevation of this Seat, with the Plans of the principal and Ground Floors, are given in the Fifth Volume of the *Vitruvius Britannicus*.

D. Molton del.

W. Watts sculp.

Clumber Park *in Nottinghamshire, the* Seat *of the* Duke *of* Newcastle,

Publish'd as the Act directs May 1st 1781, by William Watts, Chelsea.

PLATE XXIX.

CLUMBER-PARK, in NOTTINGHAMSHIRE,

The Seat of his Grace the Duke of NEWCASTLE.

(Drawn by T. MALTON, jun.)

THE Houfe ftands in a noble Park, in the Foreft of *Sherwood*, about four Miles from *Workfop*, and fix from *Retford*, in *Nottingham-shire*. The whole Building is of Stone, and neatly finifhed, from Defigns by the late Mr. *Stephen Wright*. The Apartments are large and well proportioned, furnifhed with Tafte and Elegance, and decorated with an exceeding fine Collection of Paintings, many of which are by the firft Mafters.

The Park contains a very large Track of Ground, being upwards of fourteen Miles in Circumference, which having been almoft ftripped of its magnificent Woods by former Poffeffors, has been re-planted by the prefent Duke, in fuch a Manner as will probably in Time reftore it to more than its original Beauty.

In the Environs of *Clumber-Park*, are the noble Seats of the Dukes of *Norfolk*, *Portland*, and *Kingfton*, which, with their furrounding Gardens and Plantations, are no inconfiderable Addition to the Beauty of the adjacent Profpects.

W. Watts delin.t et sculpsit.

Chifwick Houfe in Middlefex, the Seat of the Duke of Devonfhire.

Published as the Act directs May 1.1781. by W. Watts, Chelsea.

PLATE XXX.

CHISWICK-HOUSE,

In *MIDDLESEX,*

A Seat of his Grace the Duke of DEVONSHIRE.

CHISWICK, is a pleafant Village on the Banks of the *Thames,* about fix Miles South Weft of *London,* celebrated for a beautiful Villa, built by the late Earl of *Burlington,* which for Grandeur and Elegance is not furpaffed by any in the Kingdom. It has indeed, been faid, that the Edifice is too fmall (being only feventy Feet fquare, exclufive of the Portico) for fo capital and fuperb a Defign; but notwithftanding its Inferiority in this Refpect, from the agreeable Proportions and Richnefs of the Decorations, it has a moft magnificent and auguft Appearance, and is a ftriking Inftance of the great Abilities and refined Tafte of that illuftrious Architect.

The Gardens are ornamented with a Variety of Temples, Obelifks, Statues, &c. and are laid out in a moft incomparable Style. On defcending from the Back (or Garden) Front, you enter a verdant Lawn, planted with Clumps of Cypreffes and Firs, in Rows, between which are large Stone Vafes. At the Ends or Extremities of the Lawn are Lions and other Beafts on Pedeftals, well executed by *Scheemaker,* and the View is terminated by three fine antique Statues brought from *Rome,* which are relieved by a clofe Plantation of different Evergreens.

On turning from the Houfe on the Right Hand, an open Grove of Foreft Trees affords a View of the Orangery, which is feen as perfectly as if the Trees were planted on the Lawn; and when the Orange Trees are in Flower, their Fragrance is diffufed over the whole Lawn to the Houfe: Thefe are feparated from the Lawn by a Foffee, to prevent their being injured by the Company admitted to walk in the Gardens.

From the Weft-front of the Building, an eafy Slope planted with Evergreens, leads down to the Serpentine River, from whence you have a Picturefque View of the Grotto and Cafcade. Acrofs the River is an elegant Stone Bridge, adorned with Statues, &c. and on each Side are verdant Walks, which by accompanying the River in its winding Courfe, afford the greateft Variety of Profpects, uncommonly beautiful and romantic. With the Earth dug from the Bed of this River, Lord *Burlington* raifed a Terrace that commands a pleafing View of the River *Thames* and adjacent Country.

It is fomewhat remarkable that no Perfons are admitted to fee this Place without Tickets for that Purpofe, a Ceremony, we believe, not obferved at any other Seat in the Kingdom; and that upon Admiffion you are prohibited from making any Drawings. The Author of this Publication, unacquainted with thefe Particulars, met with very difagreeable Treatment, in confequence of having taken fome Sketches of the Building. This illiberal Injunction is the more extraordinary, as Plans and Elevations of the Houfe have been publifhed many Years fince by *Kent*.

G. Barrett R.A. del.

J. W. Watts sculp.

Trentham *in Staffordshire, the* Seat *of* Earl Gower.

Published as the Act directs, May 1st 1701, by W. Watts, Kemp's Row, Chelsea.

PLATE XXXI.

TRENTHAM-HALL, in STAFFORDSHIRE,

The Seat of the Right Honourable Earl G O W E R,

(Drawn by G. BARRET, Efq. R. A. from a Sketch by Enfign PLUMRIDGE.)

TRENTHAM-HALL, is an ancient and extenfive Building, fituated near *Newcaftle Under-Line*, in *Staffordfhire*, and has long been the Refidence of the Noble Family who now poffefs it. It contains many fpacious and convenient public and private Apartments, which have been lately fitted up and ornamented by the prefent Earl, who has alfo made great Alterations and Improvements throughout the whole Place, under the Direction of Meffrs. *Brown* and *Holland*. The Park is watered by the River *Trent*, and affords a great Variety of Ground, Water, and Wood, upon a very large Scale. The Kitchen Gardens are complete, and the Pleafure Grounds in the moft elegant Difpofition.

S. Hearne del.   W. Watts sculp.

Corsham House *in Wiltshire*, *the Seat of* Paul Methuen *Esq.*

Published as the Act directs, May 1.st 1781, by W. Watts, Kemp's Row, Chelsea.

PLATE XXXII.

CORSHAM-HOUSE,

In *WILTSHIRE*,

The Seat of PAUL METHUEN, Efq.

(Drawn by T. HEARNE, from a Sketch, by the Rev. Mr. GOOCH.)

THIS Edifice is fituated about four Miles from *Chippenham*, and ten from *Bath*, in a moft agreeable Part of *Wiltfhire*, much efteemed for the Salubrity of its Air. The Palace of *Ethelred*, one of the *Saxon* Kings, and after the Conqueft the Retiring Place of the Earls of *Cornwall*, ftood near the Site of the prefent Manfion, which appears, from an Infcription on the South Front, to have been built in the Year 1582. In the laft Century it was one of the Seats of Sir *Edward Hungerford*, fince which it has been much enlarged and improved, particularly by its prefent Owner, who has added an Apartment feventy Feet in Length, twenty-four in Width, and twenty-four high, for the Reception of Part of his valuable Collection of Pictures. The Park and Gardens afford from the principal Apartments, very picturefque and beautiful Profpects; and are remarkable for their rich Soil and fine Verdure.

Milton Abbey *in Dorsetshire, the* Seat *of* Lord Milton.

Published as the Act directs, Sep. 3, 1781, by W. Watts, Chelsea.

PLATE XXXIII.

MILTON ABBEY,

In *DORSETSHIRE*,

The Seat of the Right Honourable Lord MILTON,

(Drawn by the Right Honourable Lord Vifcount CARLOW.)

Milton Abbey is fituated about fix Miles from *Blandford* in *Dorfetfhire*, and was originally built by King *Athelftan*, who upon falfe Suggeftions that his Brother *Edwin* was concerting Meafures to deftroy him, caufed him to be fent to Sea in an open Boat, with only one Attendant, where being drowned, the King, repenting of his Crime, founded this Abbey to atone for it.

At the Diffolution of the Monafteries, King *Henry* VIII. granted it to Sir *John Tregonwell*, and having in Procefs of Time come into Lord *Milton*'s Poffeffion, his Lordfhip, in 1771, pulled down all the Abbey, except the noble old Hall, and raifed the prefent beautiful Structure of Portland Stone on its Scite, in a Form expreffive of its Name and former Application, and in a Style of Architecture correfponding to the venerable Church by its Side.

It ftands on a Knole backed by a high wooded Hill, at the Junction of three fpacious Vallies, which winding between other Hills covered with extenfive Plantations, give the Place a Character of Beauty peculiar to itfelf, and form the moft grand and fingular Scenes that can be conceived.

The Abbey is connected by an inclofed Arcade to the Church, which is a large and magnificent Pile of *Gothic* Architecture.

The Village formerly ftood on the South Side of the Church; but, interfering with the Plan of Improvement, has been removed to a picturefque Valley, half a Mile diftant, where it is rebuilt in a very elegant Manner.

W. Watts delin. et sculp.

Tehidy Park *in Cornwall, the* Seat *of* Sir Francis Bassett Bar.t

Published as the Act directs, Sep.t 5.th 1781, by W. Watts, Chelsea.

PLATE XXXIV.

TEHIDY PARK,

In the County of CORNWALL,

The Seat of Sir FRANCIS BASSETT, Bart.

Tehidy Park has been the Refidence of the Family of the *Baſſetts* upwards of five hundred Years; it came into their Poſſeſſion by the Marriage of *William Baſſett*, to *Cecilia*, Daughter and Heireſs of *Alan de Dunſtanville*, about the year 1200.

The Houſe is ſituated in a romantic Country, about a Mile and a half from the *Briſtol* Channel: it was erected in the Year 1736, by the Uncle of the preſent Owner, and though not large, is a convenient and well built modern Structure.

W.ᵗ Watts delin.ᵗ et sculp.ᵗ

The Seat of Sir Charles Afgill Bar.ᵗ near Richmond in SURRY.

Published as the Act directs, Sep.ᵗ 1781, by W.ᵗ Watts, Chelsea.

PLATE XXXV.

The Seat of Sir CHARLES ASGILL, Bart.

Near RICHMOND in SURRY.

The Seat of Sir *Charles Asgill*, Bart. is pleasantly situated on the Banks of the *Thames* near *Richmond* in *Surry*, and commands the most agreeable Prospects of the River *Thames* and the adjacent Country ; it was designed and built by *Robert Tayler*, Esq. and is remarkable for its elegant Simplicity.

The Plan and Elevation of this Seat is given in the *Vitruvius Brittannicus.*

W. Repton del.   W. Watts sculp.

Beeston Hall *in Norfolk, the Seat of* Jacob Preston *Esq*.

Published as the Act directs, Sep.ʳ 3.ᵈ 1781, by W. Watts, Chelsea.

PLATE XXXVI.

BEESTON HALL,

(In NORFOLK.)

The Seat of JACOB PRESTON, Esq.

(Drawn by HUMPHREY REPTON of SUSTEAD, Esq.)

Beeston Hall is situated about ten Miles North East of *Norwich*, in the Center of a well-wooded and watered Park, which, though it wants the Advantage of distant Prospect, is not without picturesque Points of View within itself. The House is large and irregular, but contains some good Apartments.

This Place formerly belonged to Sir *Robert de Norwich*, who had very extensive Possessions in this Part of the County, but has for about an hundred and fifty Years been the Residence of the present Family, and has lately been much improved.

_____ Brooke pinx.ᵗ

W. Watts sculp.

Southill *in Bedfordshire the Seat of* Lord Viscount Torrington.

Publish'd as the Act directs, Jan.ʸ 1.ᵗ 1782. by W. Watts, Chelsea.

PLATE XXXVII.

S O U T H I L L,

In *B E D F O R D S H I R E,*

The Seat of the Right Honourable Lord Viscount T O R R I N G T O N,

(Painted by Mr. B R O O K S.)

T H E House at *Southill* in *Bedfordshire,* was erected by George Viscount *Torrington,* Grandfather of the present noble Possessor; and is a roomy and convenient Structure, with good Offices. It stands three Miles from *Bigglesswade,* and about forty-four from *London,* on a dry, sandy Soil, commanding pleasant and extensive Prospects.

The Gardens at this Place were formerly very large, and held in high Estimation at the Time straight Lines and Yew Hedges were so generally approved of; but they have been materially altered, in Conformity to the present improved Taste.

W. Watts del. et sculp.

Melton Constable *in Norfolk, the Seat of* Sir Edw.d Astley Bar.t

Publish'd as the Act directs, Jan.y 1.st 1782, by W. Watts, Kemp's Row, Chelsea.

PLATE XXXVIII.

MELTON CONSTABLE,

(In N O R F O L K,)

The Seat of Sir E D W A R D   A S T L E Y, Bart.

MELTON CONSTABLE was brought into the Poffeffion of the *Aftleys*, of *Hill-Morton* in *Warwickfhire*, in the Reign of *Henry* III. by the Marriage of *Thomas* Lord *Aftley* with *Editha*, the furviving Heirefs of the refpectable Family of *Con-ftable*, whofe Refidence this Place had been for many Years before that Period. —- His Lordfhip was afterwards killed in the Barons' Wars, at *Evefham* in *Worcefterfhire*.

The Houfe, as well as the Place in general, has undergone various and material Changes. The old Building was pulled down, and the prefent Structure raifed by Sir *Jacob Aftley*, Knight and Baronet, about the Year 1680. The Apartments are large and well proportioned, and have been elegantly furnifhed by the prefent Owner, Sir *Edward Aftley*; who has, like-wife, at a great Expence, new modelled and ornamented the Grounds, under the Direction of *Lancelot Brown*, Efq. with a Variety of Plantations, a fpacious Lake, and a curious Menagerie. It is fituated about nine Miles from *Fakenham*, in the Middle of an extenfive Park, well ftocked with Deer, and commands uninterrupted Profpects over a cultivated and beauti-ful Country, bounded by the Sea on the Eaft, and extending Weftward to the Spires of *Norwich*, which may be feen dif-tinctly, in a clear Day, at the Diftance of twenty Miles.

W. Watts del et sculp.

Holkham *in Norfolk, the* Seat *of* Tho.* Wenman Coke *Esq.*

Published as the Act directs Jan 7.* 1782, by W. Watts, Chelsea.

PLATE XXXIX.

HOLKHAM-HOUSE,

(In NORFOLK,)

The Seat of THOMAS WENMAN COKE, Efq.

THE general Ideas of *Holkham-Houfe* were firft ftruck out by the Earls of *Leicefter* and *Burlington*, affifted by Mr. *Kent*, who had been encouraged in his Studies at *Rome* by the joint Patronage of thofe Noblemen, and afterwards brought to Perfection by Mr. *Brettingham*, of *Norwich*, under whofe Infpection the Work was executed.

The Building confifts of a Center and four Wings, one at each Angle; the Center is quadrangular, 160 feet by 115, and has a Communication with the Wings, by rectilinear Corridors. It extends, including the Wings, 345 feet, and is 180 in depth, forming four different Fronts, of which the North and South are particularly beautiful, and in the moft perfect and chafte Style of Architecture. The South Front has a fine Portico of eight Corinthian Columns; but the Entrance has not fufficient Grandeur to correfpond ftrictly with the other Parts of the Compofition, and is certainly too diminutive for fuch a magnificent Pile of Building.

The Earl of *Leicefter*, amidft the Improvements of Planting and Agriculture carried on with Succefs at *Holkham*, omitted no Opportunity of improving and decorating this Villa, his favourite Object. Befides attending to the interior Embellifhments of Paintings and Statues, which he had begun to collect during his Refidence at *Rome*, he continued with uncommon Diligence to improve and elucidate the firft Sketches, in Concert with the Earl of *Burlington* and Mr. *Kent*; and in this he was guided chiefly by *Palladio* and *Inigo Jones*.

The Idea of the great Hall was formed from the Example of a Bafilica, or Court of Juftice, by *Palladio*, and exhibited in his Defigns for *Barbaro*'s Tranflation of *Vitruvius*. It extends 70 feet by 46, and is ornamented with 18 fluted *Ionic* Columns of variegated Marble, taken from *Degodetz*'s Meafures of the Temple of *Fortuna Virilis* at *Rome*.

The

The Statue Gallery, which is 60 feet by 21, bears a near Analogy to that in the Earl of *Burlington*'s elegant Villa at *Chifwick**, (evidently taken, though with fome Deviation, from the Marchefe *Capri*'s, built by *Andrea Palladio*, near the Town of *Vicenza*,) and contains a fine Collection of antique Statues, Bufts, &c. The Saloon, with the Reft of the State Apartments, are likewife finifhed and decorated in the moft fuperb Tafte. The Chimney-Pieces are of Jafper, Porphyry, Siena, and other Marbles. The Cielings and Entablatures are ornamented. The Hangings are of Silk, Velvet, and Tapeftry; and the Pictures, of which there is a noble Collection, are by the firft Mafters.

The South Front of this celebrated Manfion will probably appear in the Courfe of this Publication, with fome further Particulars.

* Now the Duke of *Devonfhire*'s.

J.t.Grefse del.   W.Watts sculp.

Cannons *in Middlesex, the* Seat of W.ᵐ Hallett *Esqʳ*

Published as the Act directs Janʸ.1.ˢᵗ1782, by W.Watts, Chelsea.

PLATE XL.

C A N N O N S,

In MIDDLESEX,

The Seat of WILLIAM HALLETT, Esq.

(Drawn by J. A. GRESSE.)

THIS Manfion is fituated near *Edgware*, in *Middlefex*, precifely on the fame Scite the magnificent Palace of *James* Duke of *Chandos* formerly ftood. It was built by Mr. *Hallett*, who purchafed the faid Duke's Eftate at this Place, in or about the Year 1747.

The prefent Edifice, though not very extenfive, being only a Square of about fifty Feet, is neverthelefs an elegant and commodious Refidence. The whole Building is of Stone; the Offices are made under-ground, the Cellars of the former Houfe having been appropriated for that Purpofe. The old Afpects have alfo been retained in the Superftructure, and command pleafant rifing Views, three feveral Ways.

The Grounds, which were before adorned with Viftas and other grand Decorations, in the Tafte of thofe Times, have been judicioufly modelled into a pleafing Park, by the prefent Owner, who is gradually improving the Eftate, both in Beauty and Value.

*** For any Particulars refpecting the former State of this Place, the Reader is referred to *Dodfley's Environs of London*.

A. Devis del.   W. Watts sculp.

West-Front of **Burghley-House** in Northamptonshire, the Seat of the Earl of **Exeter**.

Publish'd as the Act directs, May 1.st 1782, by W. Watts, Chelsea.

PLATE XLI.

WEST FRONT of BURGHLEY HOUSE,

In *NORTHAMPTONSHIRE*;

The Seat of the Right Honourable the Earl of EXETER.

(*Drawn by A. DEVIS.*)

A GENERAL Engraving of *Burghley* was given in the fixth Number of this Publication; but, we apprehend, a fecond Plate of fo celebrated a Place, exhibited in a nearer Point of View, by the fame Artift, will not be unacceptable to our Subfcribers.

For the Defcription fee Plate XXI.

 S. Sandby R. A. del.

W. Watts sculp.

Glames - Castle *in Scotland, the* Seat *of the* Earl *of* Strathmore.

Published as the Act directs, May 1.st 1782, by W. Watts, Chelsea.

PLATE XLII.

GLAMES CASTLE,

In SCOTLAND;

The Seat of the Earl of STRATHMORE.

(Drawn by T. SANDBY, Esq. R. A.)

GLAMES CASTLE is a Place celebrated in History, particularly for the Murder of *Malcolm* II. who fell here by the Hands of Assassins, in a Passage, which is still shewn to Strangers. It might have been at that Time Part of the Possessions of the Family of *Macbeth*, since he observes, according to *Shakespeare*,

"By *Sinel's* Death I know I'm Thane of *Glames*,"

This *Sinel*, as *Boethius* informs us, was Father to that Tyrant: Probably after his Death it became forfeited, and added to the Property of the Crown; for, on the Accession of *Robert* II. it was bestowed (then a royal Palace) on his Favourite, Sir *John Lyon*, *Propter laudabili et fideli servitio, et continuis laboribus.* The ancient Structure was of great Extent: It consisted of two long Courts, divided by Buildings; in each was a square Tower, and Gateway beneath; and in the third another Tower, which constitutes the present House, the Rest being totally destroyed. This has received many Alterations, by the Additions of little round Turrets, with grotesque Roofs; and by a great round Tower, in one Angle, which was built in 1686, by the Restorer of the Castle, *Patrick* Lord *Glames*, in Order to contain the curious Stair-case, which is spiral; one End of the Steps resting on a light hollow Pillar, continued to the upper Story. The most spacious Rooms are, as is usual in similar Buildings, placed in the upper Part, and furnished with all the tawdry and clumsy Magnificence of the Middle of the last Century. The habitable Part is below Stairs.

Glames Castle is situated in the Vale of *Strathmore*, between *Perth* and *Brechin*, and is about six Miles north of *Forfar*, in the eastern Part of *Scotland*.

The above Description is extracted from Mr. Pennant's Tour, Vol. III.

T. Hearne del.   W. Watts sculp.

Heveningham Hall *in Suffolk, the Seat of* Sir Gerard W.m Vanneck Bar.t

Published as the Act directs May 1.1782, by W. Watts, Chelsea.

PLATE XLIII.

HEVENINGHAM HALL,

In SUFFOLK;

The Seat of Sir GERARD WILLIAM VANNECK, Bart.

(Drawn by T. HEARNE, in 1780.)

FROM the earlieſt Accounts of *Heveningham*, we learn that the Lordſhip was poſſeſſed by *Walter Fitz-Robert* in the laſt Year of King Richard I. It was afterwards, for many Generations, in a Family whoſe Name was derived from the Place, but whether deſcended from *Fitz-Robert* or not is uncertain. In the Beginning of the preſent Century it became the Eſtate of *John Bence*, Eſq. by whoſe immediate Heir it was ſold into the Family of *Daſhwood*, from which it paſſed to the *Damers*. The Lordſhip and Eſtate are now in the Poſſeſſion of Sir *Gerard Vanneck*, Bart. who converted the old Manor-Houſe into the preſent magnificent Structure. It ſtands on an eaſy Slope, backed by large Trees, with extended Plantations of Oak, Beech, Fir and other Timber; and commands cheerful Proſpects, beautifully varied, particularly towards the Eaſt and Weſt. The River *Blythe*, which runs eaſtward through the Valley, ſpreads itſelf into a large Sheet of Water, within View of the ſeveral Apartments, and is navigable from the Port of *Southwold* to the ancient Market-Town of *Haleſworth*, within four Miles of this Seat, near the *Roman* Way from the *Villa Fauſtini* ＊ to *Caſter*, a military Station at the Confluence of the *Yare* and the *Waveney*.

The Lands of *Heveningham* are generally rich and fertile, diverſified by Inequality of Ground, Woods, Tilth, and Paſturage. The Houſe is ſituated in a pleaſant Park, near the great Road from *London* to *Yarmouth*, and its Diſtance from the Sea is about ten Miles, through a fine ſporting Country, abounding with Game.

The annexed Plate exhibits the North Aſpect of the Building, which is remarked, not only for the Grandeur and Elegance of its Apartments, but the Convenience of their Diſpoſition for the Purpoſes of Hoſpitality, by which its Owner is eminently diſtinguiſhed.

＊ Now St. Edmund's Bury.

J. Hearne del.   *W. Watts sculp.*

Weſtwick *in Norfolk, the Seat of* John Berney Petre *Eſq.ʳ*

Publiſh'd as the Act directs, May 1.ˢᵗ 1782, by W. Watts, Chelſea.

PLATE XLIV.

WESTWICK,

In NORFOLK;

The Seat of JOHN BERNEY PETRE, Esq.

(Drawn by T. HEARNE, from a Sketch by H. REPTON, Esq.)

WESTWICK is situated twelve Miles from *Norwich*, and three from *North Walsham*. It is deservedly esteemed one of the most delightful Spots in the County of *Norfolk*; the most judicious and happy Efforts of Art having laid open and displayed, in a most agreeable Manner, the natural Beauties of the Place. The Kitchen-Garden and Hot-houses are inferior to few or none in this Part of the Kingdom. The Lawn and Plantations are extensive and beautiful. It was long thought impracticable to obtain an ornamental Piece of Water for the farther Improvement of the Scene, on Account of the elevated Situation of the Place, and the Nature of the Soil: but that Difficulty is at last fully surmounted; Mr. Petre having been able, by an ingenious Application of two Archimedean Screws, to raise a sufficient Supply from a large Reservoir below to the Summit of the Hill. These Screws are worked by a Windmill, and will discharge above 500 Barrels an Hour when the Wind is brisk. The lower Screw raises the Water eleven Feet, into a Cistern, from which the other takes it eleven Feet higher, into a Channel made for the Conveyance of it to its Place of Destination. This Channel winds along near three Miles; sometimes through Hills, where it is fourteen or fifteen Feet deep; and sometimes over low Grounds, where it is elevated to a considerable Height above the Surface of the Earth. The Water, when finished, will be upwards of a Mile in Length, and will complete the Beauty of the Lawn and Plantations.

At a little Distance from the House is an ornamental Building, or Gazebo, erected some Years since by Mr. *Petre*, remarkable for the fine Prospect it affords: It takes in a large Extent of the Sea-coast on one Side; and on the other, a rich inland Country, as far as the Eye can reach; the Whole in the highest State of Cultivation, and most beautifully cloathed with Wood.

T. Hearne del.

W. Watts sculp.

Charlton-House in Wiltshire, the Seat of the Earl of Suffolk.

Published as the Act directs, Sep.r 1.st 1782. by W. Watts, Chelsea.

PLATE XLV.

CHARLTON HOUSE,

In *WILTSHIRE*.

The Seat of the Right Honourable The Earl of SUFFOLK,

(Drawn by T. HEARNE, from a Sketch by RICHARD CARTER, Efq.)

T H E annexed Plate reprefents the Eaft Front of the Building, which is of Stone, Quadrangular, and very large, extending one hundred and twenty eight Feet by one hundred and eighty. The late Earl re-built two entire Fronts of the Houfe, and fo materially altered the whole interior Part that it may be faid to be new; thefe Improvements were made under the Direction of *Matthew Brettingham*, Efq. Architect, and not wholly completed at the Time of his Lordfhip's Death, which happened in the year 1779.

The Weft Front is faid to have been defigned by *Inigo Jones*. The principal Apartments are large and elegant: the Hall which occupies the Centre of the Building, is fixty three Feet by fifty three, and forty in Height; the Dining Room is forty five by twenty four: the Drawing Room, thirty eight by twenty four, and the Library thirty eight by twenty.

Charlton Houfe is fituate near the Town of *Malmfbury*.

W. Watts del. et Sculp.t

Houghton *in Norfolk, the* Seat *of the* Earl *of* Orford.

Published as the Act directs, Sep.r 1.t 1782, by W. Watts, Chelsea.

PLATE XLVI.

HOUGHTON,

In NORFOLK;

The Seat of the Right Honourable the Earl of ORFORD.

HOUGHTON, one of the moſt celebrated Edifices in *England*, was begun by Sir *Robert Walpole*, in the Year 1722, and compleated in 1735, as appears from the following Inſcription over the South-end Door, which is the common Approach to the Houſe. " *Robertus Walpole, Has Ædes, Anno S.* MDCCXXII. *Inchoavit, Anno* MDCCXXXV. *Perfecit.*" It ſtands five Miles from *Fakenham*, in a fine Park, and is ſurrounded by magnificent and extenſive Plantations, which form a Circumference of about eight Miles. The whole Building is of Stone, and though not ſtrictly conformable to the preſent Taſte in ſome Particulars, is, nevertheleſs, a ſuperb and elegant Structure. It extends, including the Wings, which contain the Offices, 500 Feet. The Center is 165 Feet by 100, and conſiſts of a ruſtic, principal, and attic Story, terminated at the four Angles by Cupolas; the Weſt Front is ornamented with a Pediment, containing the Arms of the Family, ſupported by four *Ionic* three-quarter Columns, and is crowned with Statues. The Entrance was originally in the principal Story, by a grand Flight of Steps in each Front, but is now confined to the Baſement, (ſimilar to *Holkham)* the Steps having been lately pulled down, in Conſequence of their being conſiderably decayed.

The principal Apartments at *Houghton* are the following. The Saloon, 40 Feet long, 40 high, and 30 wide; the Hangings of Crimſon flowered Velvet; the Cieling painted by *Kent*, who deſigned all the Ornaments throughout the Houſe; the Chimneypiece, as well as the Tables, are of black and gold Marble.—The Hall is a Cube of 40 Feet, with a Stone Gallery round three Sides; the Cieling and Frieze by *Altari*; the Figures over the Doors by *Ryſbrack*. — The Drawing-room is 30 Feet by 21, hung with yellow Caffoy, and adorned with ſome fine Carving by *Gibbins*. — The *Carlo-Maratt* Room (ſo called from its being formerly hung with Pictures by that Maſter) is of the ſame Dimenſions; the Hangings are green Velvet; the Tables of *Lapis Lazuli*; at each End are Sconces of maſſive Silver.—The common Parlour is alſo 30 Feet by 21, and contains ſome Carving by *Gibbins*. — The Marble-parlour is 30 Feet by 24; one entire Side of the Room is Marble, with Alcoves for Side-boards, ſupported by columns of *Ply-*

mouth

mouth Marble ; over the Chimney is a fine Piece of *Alto Rellevo*, by *Ryſbrack*.—The Library is 21 Feet by 22, as is alſo the Cabinet. — The Gallery (which is in the right hand Wing) is 71 long, 21 wide, and 21 high ; the Hangings of *Norwich* Damaſk. It was originally intended for a Green-houſe ; but, on Sir *Robert Walpole*'s Reſignation in 1742, it was fitted up for the Pictures which were in *Downing-ſtreet.*

The capital Paintings which formerly ornamented theſe Apartments, and which unqueſtionably formed the fineſt Collection in the Kingdom, except the royal one, we are ſorry to obſerve, are now in the Poſſeſſion of the *Empreſs* of *Ruſſia*, who, it is ſaid, has lately purchaſed them for 40000l.

W. Watts del. et sculp.

Seat of Sir Gregory Page Turner Bar.t at Blackheath in Kent.

Published as the Act directs, Octor. 7th. 1782, by W. Watts, Chelsea.

PLATE XLVII.

The Seat of Sir GREGORY PAGE TURNER, Bart.

At BLACK-HEATH, in KENT.

THIS Edifice is situated near *Morden-College*, on the South-east Extremity of *Blackheath*. It was built by the late Sir *Gregory Page*, and bequeathed by him, at his Decease, to his Nephew Sir *Gregory Turner*, of *Ambroseden* in *Oxfordshire*; who has taken the Name and Arms of *Page*, in Compliance with his Uncle's Request; but not residing here, it has lately been let to different Possessors. It stands in a pleasant Park, with a small Piece of Water before each Front, and commands fine Prospects, particularly to the South and East, over *Shooter's-Hill, Eltham,* and the adjacent Country. The Center of the Building consists of a Basement, State, and Attic Story, terminated by an elegant Balustrade, and adorned to the South with a noble *Ionic* Portico; the Ascent to which is by semi-circular Flights of Steps. The Wings are very extensive, projecting two hundred Feet from the North Front, at Right Angles; they contain the Offices, Stables, &c. and have a Communication with the House by Colonades, but from their Disproportion to the Center, and dissimilar Stile, have not the most agreeable Effect. The whole Fabrick is of Stone, and is remarkable (considering its Extent) for having been covered in the Space of eleven Months from the Time it was begun. — At this Seat are some capital Paintings by *Rubens, Vandyke. P. Veronese, N. Poussin, Titian,* and other admired Masters.

W. Watts del. et sculp.

Seat of the R.t Hon. Welbore Ellis, at Twickenham in Middlesex.

Published as the Act directs Octo.r 5.t 1782, by W. Watts, Chelsea.

PLATE XLVIII.

The Seat of the Right Honourable WELBORE ELLIS,

At TWICKENHAM, in MIDDLESEX.

THIS Villa is delightfully fituated on the Banks of the *Thames*, at *Twickenham*, and is particularly memorable for having been the Refidence of Mr. *Pope*, who purchafed it in the Year 1715, and improved it with fo much Tafte and Elegance, that it became an Object of general Admiration. The Houfe and Gardens have, however, been confiderably enlarged fince, by the late Sir *William Stanhope*, who purchafed them after the Death of that celebrated Poet.

One of the chief Ornaments of this agreeable Retreat was the Grotto, the Improvement of which was the favourite Amufement of Mr. *Pope's* declining Years; fo that not long before his Death, by enlarging and enriching it with a number of curious Ores and Minerals, he made it one of the moft elegant and romantic Retirements, in accomplifhing which he was affifted by Prefents of various Kinds from feveral of his Friends, procured from different Quarters of the Globe.

It may not be improper to add the Defcription Mr. *Pope* himfelf gave of this romantic Spot, in a Letter to a Friend. " I have," fays he, " put the laft Hand to my Works of this Kind, in happily finifhing the fubterranean Way and Grotto: I there found a " Spring of the cleareft Water, which falls in a perpetual Rill, that echoes through the Cavern Day and Night. From the River " *Thames* you fee through the Arch, up a Walk of the Wildernefs, to a Kind of open Temple, wholly compofed of Shells, in the " ruftic Manner; and from that Diftance, under the Temple, you look down through a floping Arcade of Trees, and fee the Sails " on the River paffing fuddenly and vanifhing, as through a perfpective Glafs. When you fhut the Doors of this Grotto, it be- " comes on the Inftant, from a luminous Room, a *Camera obfcura*, on the Walls of which all the Objects of the River, Hills, Woods, " and Boats, are forming a moving Picture in their vifible Radiations; and when you have a Mind to light it up, it affords you a " very different Scene; it is finifhed with Shells, interfperfed with Pieces of Looking-glafs in regular Forms; and on the " Cieling is a Star of the fame Material, at which when a Lamp (of an orbicular Figure, of thin Alabafter) is hung in the Middle,

a thoufand

" a thoufand pointed rays glitter, and are reflected over the Place. There are connected to this Grotto, by a narrow Paffage, two
" Porches, one towards the River, of fmooth Stones, full of Light, and open ; the other towards the Garden, fhadowed with
" Trees, rough with Shells, Flints, and Iron-ore. The Bottom is paved with fimple Pebbles, as is alfo the adjoining Walk up the
" Wildernefs to the Temple, in the natural Tafte, agreeing not ill with the little dripping Murmur, and the aquatic Idea of the
" whole Place."

This admired Spot is now in the Poffeffion of the Right Honourable *Welbore Ellis*, who married the Daughter of the late
Sir *William Stanhope*; and at prefent receives a confiderable Addition to its Beauty, from the drooping Willows on the Margin
of the River, which are faid to be the fineft in the Kingdom.

W. Watts, del. et Sculp.

Sion House *in Middlesex the* Seat *of the* Duke *of* Northumberland.

Published as the Act directs Feby 1st 1783 by W. Watts, Chelsea.

PLATE XLIX.

SION HOUSE,

In *MIDDLESEX,*

The Seat of his Grace the Duke of NORTHUMBERLAND.

SION HOUSE was originally a Convent, founded by *Henry V.* for Nuns of the Order of St. *Bridget,* but after the Diffo-lution of the Monafteries, was granted to the Protector Duke of *Somerfet,* who built a Palace here out of the Ruins, the Shell of which yet remains unaltered. Upon the Fall of that Nobleman it reverted to the Crown, but was afterwards obtained by *Henry Percy,* ninth Earl of *Northumberland,* from whom it has defcended to the prefent illuftrious Poffeffor.—The Houfe ftands exactly on the fame Spot where the Church belonging to the Monaftery formerly ftood, and is a large majeftic Structure, built of white Stone. It has four extenfive Fronts, with a Tower at each Angle, flat-roofed like the Reft of the Building, and furrounded with Battle-ments. The grand Approach is from the Weftern Road, through an elegant Gateway, with an open Colonade on each Side, lately erected (from the Defigns of Mr. *Adam)* by the prefent Duke, who has made furprizing Improvements throughout the whole Place. The great Hall is an oblong Apartment, ornamented with antique Marble Coloffal Statues: it was finifhed nearly as it now appears by *Inigo Jones,* who made feveral Alterations in different Parts of the Houfe. From the Hall a Flight of Marble Steps leads to the Veftibule, which is fquare, and finifhed in an uncommon Style: the Floor is of *Scaglioli,* and the Walls in fine Relief, with gilt Trophies and other Ornaments: in this Room are twelve large Columns and fixteen Pilafters of *Verde antique.* The Dining-room is decorated with Marble Statues and Paintings in *Chiaro obfcuro,* after the antique: at each End is a circular Recefs, feparated by gilt Columns; the Cieling is in Stucco, gilt. This leads to the Drawing-room, which is hung with a rich three-coloured Damafk, being the firft of the Kind ever executed in *England*: the Tables are antique Mofaic, found in *Titus's* Baths; the Glaffes are thirteen Feet by five and a half; the Chimney-piece is of Statuary Marble, inlaid with *Or Moulû*; and the Cieling, which is coved and divided into fmall Compartments, gilt, exhibits Defigns of antique Paintings well executed. The Gallery is one hundred and thirty-three Feet in Length, enriched, likewife, with antique Painting and Ornaments: this Room opens at the Eaft End into a Suite of private Apartments, which lead back to the great Hall.

The

The Gardens at *Sion* have likewise been improved with an equal Degree of Taste and Elegance: they were originally laid out by the Protector *Somerset*, but at a Time when extensive Views were judged to be inconsistent with that solemn Reserve and stately Privacy usually affected by the great, and were so ill contrived as to deprive the House of every Prospect the Neighbourhood afforded: to remedy this Inconvenience, the Garden Wall, as well as an high Terrace, which had been raised at a great Expence, have been removed, and the Ground levelled: by these Means a fine Lawn is formed, extending from *Isleworth* to *Brentford*, and a delightful Prospect opened into the royal Gardens at *Richmond*, as well as up and down the River *Thames*, the Surface of the Water being now visible even from the lower Apartments. His Grace has not only thus improved the Ground where the Gardens formerly were situated, but has also made a very large Addition to it, and separated the two Parts by a serpentine River, which communicates with the *Thames*, and is adorned with two handsome Bridges.

Chifwick House *in Middlefex, the* Seat *of the* Duke *of* Devonshire.

Publifhed as the Act directs Feb.y 1st 1783 by W. Watts, Chelsea.

W. Watts del. et Sculp.

PLATE L.

CHISWICK HOUSE,

In *MIDDLESEX*,

The Seat of His Grace The Duke of DEVONSHIRE.

A VIEW of the Garden Front of this elegant Seat was given in the eighth Number of this Publication, * with a Defcription of the Place, but from the Originality and Beauty of the Subject we are induced to offer a fecond Plate, accompanied with fome farther Particulars.

An Avenue formed by two Rows of ftately Cedars of *Libanus* leads to the Houfe, and produces an Effect uncommonly ftriking and beautiful, the dark Teint of thefe folemn Evergreens affording a pleafing Contraft to the Whitenefs of the Building which appears between them : thefe Trees were planted by Lord *Burlington*, and are faid to be the fineft of the Kind in the Kingdom. The Entrance to the principal Story is by a double Flight of Steps, on one fide of which, is the Statue of *Palladio*, and on the other, that of *Inigo Jones*. The Columns of the Portico are of the *Corinthian* Order, fluted, with the Entablature as rich as poffible. The infide of the Structure is alfo finifhed with the utmoft Elegance ; the Cielings are richly gilt and painted ; and the Pictures, of which there is a noble Collection, are by the beft Mafters.

* See Plate XXX.

O. Malton del.

M. Watts sculp.

Wentworth Castle in Yorkshire the Seat of the Earl of Strafford.

Published as the Act directs Octr. 1st. 1783 by W. Watts Chelsea.

PLATE LI.

WENTWORTH CASTLE,

In *YORKSHIRE*,

The Seat of the Right Honourable the Earl of STRAFFORD,

(*Drawn by T. MALTON, Junior.*)

WENTWORTH CASTLE, in the Weſt Riding of the County of *York*, is ſituated about two Miles from *Barnſley*, upon an agreeable Eminence, commanding the moſt delightful Proſpects over the Village of *Worſborough* and the adjacent Country, which is very romantic and picturefque. The North Road to *Leeds* and *Harrowgate*, runs at a little Diſtance from the Houſe, and greatly enlivens the Scene, being viſible for near two Miles in different Breaks, and is finally terminated by the Summit of a ſteep Hill, called *Bank-top*: upon this Hill is an artificial Ruin of a large Caſtle, built by the preſent Earl, who has erected ſeveral emble-matical Temples and other Edifices in various Parts of the Grounds, particularly one to the Memory of the unfortunate Earl of *Strafford*, who ſuffered in the Time of *Charles* I. His Lordſhip has alſo built an entire new Front to the Houſe, which is deſervedly admired for its Lightneſs and elegant Simplicity.

The principal Apartments are ſpacious, and handſomely fitted up: the Hall is forty Feet by forty, the Cieling ſupported by *Corinthian* Pillars, and divided into Compartments, the Cornices richly worked and gilt: the Drawing-room is forty Feet by twenty-five, the Chimney-piece very beautifully finiſhed in *Siena* and Statuary Marble; here are likewiſe three fine Slabs of *Egyptian* Gra-nite and *Siena*: the Gallery is one hundred and eighty Feet long, twenty-four broad, and thirty high, divided into three Parts by magnificent Pillars of Marble, with gilt Capitals; the Cornices of the End Diviſion are alſo of Marble, richly ornamented; between the Columns are the Statues of *Apollo, Bacchus, Ceres,* and an *Ægyptian Prieſteſs*: one End of this Apartment is furniſhed for Muſic, and the other with a Billiard-table: the Library is thirty Feet by twenty: the Dining-room thirty by twenty-five; in this

Apartment

Apartment is a fine Portrait of the above-mentioned Earl of *Strafford*, by *Vandyke*. There are, likewife, feveral other good Paintings in the different Rooms, particularly *David* with the Head of *Goliah*, by *Carlo Maratti* ; two Cattle-pieces, by *Salvator Rofa* ; *Charles* I. in the Ifle of *Wight*, by *Vandyke* ; a Portrait of *Carlo Maratti*, by himfelf ; with a *Turkifh* Lady who was kept by him ; *Chrift* in the Garden, by the fame Mafter ; and a Company at Cards, by *Michael Angelo*.

This Seat is about fix Miles diftant from *Wentworth-Houfe*, the Seat of the late Marquis of *Rockingham*, a View of which was given in the fecond Number of this Work.

Rainham *in Norfolk the* Seat *of* Lord Visc.t Townshend.

Published as the Act directs Feb.y 1.st 1783 by W. Watts Chelsea.

W. Watts del.t et sculp.

PLATE LII.

R A I N H A M,

In *NORFOLK.*

The Seat of the Right Honourable Lord Viscount TOWNSHEND.

RAINHAM, the Seat of the Viscount *Townshend*, lies three Miles S. W. from *Fakenham*, in *Norfolk*. The Estate and Seat came into the noble Family of *Townshend* by the Marriage of *Lodovie de Towneshénd* with *Elizabeth* Daughter and Heiress of Sir *Thomas de Hayvile*, Knt. about the Reign of *Henry* III. or *Edward* I. since which Period it has continued with little Intermission to be the Residence of their Descendants.

The old Family House stood near the River, and was (agreeable to the Mode of those early Times) surrounded with a Moat for Defence, which is yet remaining with some Part of the Building.

In the Reign of *Charles* I. Sir *Roger Townshend*, Bart. disliking probably the low and damp Situation, or perhaps, because the Structure was then old and ruinous, built on an adjacent Eminence in the Park the present stately Mansion (as Sir *Henry Spelman* calls it) from a Plan of that famous British Architect, *Inigo Jones*. His Son *Horatio*, the First Viscount *Townshend*, in the Year 1671, entertained here *Charles* II. and the Duke of *York*, with their Court, in their Progress through the County of *Norfolk*, of which he was then Lord Lieutenant. The second Viscount, *Charles* Son of *Horatio* (many Years Secretary of State to King *George* I. and II.) greatly modernised the House, and fitted up the principal Apartments under the Direction of *Kent*; his Lordship also added a large Wing of convenient Offices, and formed the Lake in the Park. The present Viscount (his Grandson) has ornamented the adjacent Country as well as the Park with extensive Plantations, which are laid out with great Taste and Judgment, and have thriven prodigiously, the Soil being peculiarly adapted to the growth of Forest-trees of different Kinds. The Park, at present, contains about eight hun-

dred

dred Acres, but will, with the additional Ground which is fhortly intended to be thrown within the Pale, confift of near twelve hundred : the Water likewife, when compleated according to the propofed Plan, will be near two Miles in extent.

Upon the Whole we may obferve, that this Seat, though not equal in Magnificence to fome we have given in this Work, is yet a complete and defireable Refidence. The Edifice is fpacious, and remarkable for the convenient Arrangement of its Apartments ; and it poffeffes in an eminent Degree every Advantage of Soil and Situation.

We fhould not omit to mention that at *Rainham* is the very celebrated Picture of *Belifarius* by *Salvator Rofa*. There are likewife fome good Portraits of the Family, and Others.

Hatfield House in Hertfordshire, the Seat of the Earl of Salisbury.

Publish'd as the Act directs Jan.ʳ 1ˢᵗ 783 by W. W— Chelsea.

PLATE LIII.

HATFIELD HOUSE,

In *HERTFORDSHIRE*,

The Seat of the Right Honourable the Earl of SALISBURY.

THE Manor of *Hatfield* was purchafed of the See of *Ely* by Queen *Elizabeth*, who refided at the epifcopal Palace here at the Time of Queen *Mary*'s Death. Her Succeffor, King *James* I. in the fifth Year of his Reign, exchanged this Manor of *Hatfield* for *Theobalds*, in the fame County, with his Minifter Sir *Robert Cecil*, afterwards Earl of *Salifbury*, " who (on the Site of the epifcopal Palace) erected a ftately Building, which is a fair Palace, that exceeds all the " Houfes in this County, and has two large Parks, one for Fallow, the other for red Deer, with a Vineyard at the " Bottom of the Park."*

This Building is of Brick, and very large. — In the Center is an extenfive Portico of nine Arches; over the middlemoft rifes a lofty Tower, on the Front of which is the Date 1611, and three Ranges of Columns of the *Tufcan*, *Doric*, and *Compofite* Orders: Between the fecond are the Arms of the Family in Stone.

The prefent Earl of *Salifbury* has reftored this magnificent Seat of his Anceftors to its primitive Grandeur, and has at a confiderable Expence united the two Parks above mentioned, which were before feparated by the great North Road: His Lordfhip has, likewife, with much Tafte and Judgment, removed the Walls with which the Houfe was heretofore furrounded, an Improvement which has enabled us to give a View of this celebrated Place.

* Chauncey's Antiquities of Hertfordfhire, page 308.

Hon.ble C. G. Perceval, delin.

W. Watts, Sculp.

Enmore Castle in Somersetshire the Seat of the Earl of Egmont.

Published as the Act directs June 1.st 1783 by W. Watts, Chelsea.

PLATE LIV.

ENMORE CASTLE,

In *SOMERSETSHIRE*,

The Seat of the Right Honourable John James Perceval, Earl of EGMONT,

Lord Lovel and Holland, of Enmore.

(From a Drawing by the Honourable CHARLES GEORGE PERCEVAL.)

ENMORE CASTLE is fituated four Miles Weft of *Bridgwater*, in the County of *Somerfet*. It ftands on an Eminence, which commands a very noble Profpect, the View being bounded by the Mendip Hills on the Eaft, and on the South by the Hills in Glamorganfhire, which are feen very diftinctly acrofs that Part of the *Briftol* Channel in which the fteep and flat Holmes lie.

The Caftle is built round a great Court or Quadrangle, 86 Feet in Length, by 78 in Breadth, and furrounded by a dry Foffeè, 16 Feet deep, and 40 wide, on the Outfide of which is a great Range of under-ground Offices, which are lighted from the Foffeè, covered with Earth, and concealed from the Eye.

The Entrance is in the Eaft Front, through a Gateway, which is defended by a Drawbridge of a very curious Conftruction.

The Caftle was built by *John* the laft Earl of *Egmont*, who himfelf defigned and planned the Whole. — The North and South Fronts are about 157 Feet in Length, and the Eaft and Weft 150.

The Parifh Church of *Enmore* ftands in the Park, at a fmall Diftance, as it is feen in the Plate, which fhews the North and Eaft Fronts of the Caftle.

T. Hearne. del.

W. Wells, Sculp.

The Moat *in* Kent, *the Seat of* Lord Romney.

Published as the Act directs June 1st 1783 by W. Wells, Chelsea.

PLATE LV.

THE MOAT,

In KENT,

The Seat of the Right Honourable Lord ROMNEY.

(Drawn by T. HEARNE.)

THIS Place, in the Reign of *Henry* III. belonged to the Family of *Leybourn*. In the 29th Year of *Edward* III. it was in the Poffeffion of Lord *Burghurft*, Lord Warden of the Cinque Ports, who lived in the Caftle here. From the *Burghurfts* it defcended to the *Woodvilles*, as appears by a Monument in the Church at *Maidftone*. — *Richard Woodville*, in *Henry* VIth's Time, was ftiled Lord *Rivers*, *Grafton*, and *De la Moat*. — Upon the Extinction of this Family, (the feven Sons dying without Iffue) it was fold to Sir *Henry Wyat*, Privy-Counfellor to *Henry* VIII. from whom it defcended to his Grandfon, Sir *Thomas Wyat*, who forfeiting it to the Crown, it was granted by Queen *Mary* to *Hugh Warham*, who fold it to Sir *William Rither*, Lord Mayor of *London*, by whom it was repaired. His Daughter, Lady *Sufannah Cæfar*, and her eldeft Son, *Thomas Cæfar*, Efq. jointly, fold it to Sir *Humphrey Tufton*, from whofe Family it was finally purchafed by Sir *John Marfham*, Bart. created Lord *Romney* in the Year 1716, at whofe Deceafe it became the Inheritance of the prefent noble and worthy Poffeffor. —— The Houfe is fituated near *Maidftone*, in a fine Park, which contains Variety of Ground, commanding pleafant Views of the neighbouring Hills, and poffeffing the Advantages of fine Timber, rich Verdure, and an ample Supply of Water from an excellent Spring which rifes in the Garden.

W. Watts del. et Sculp

Wansted House in Essex the Seat of Earl Tylney.

Publish'd as the Act directs, June 1st 1783 by W. Watts, Chelsea.

PLATE LVI.

WANSTED HOUSE,

In ESSEX,

The Seat of the Earl of TYLNEY.

WANSTED HOUSE is situated upon the Western Part of *Epping Forest*, about six Miles North East of *London*. It was begun by Sir *Josias Child*, who purchased the Manor of *Wansted*, and finished by the late Earl *Tylney*, from Designs of *Colin Campbell*, (Author of the Vitruvius Britannicus) It extends 260 Feet by 75, and consists of a rustic Basement, and principal Story, with an Attic in the Center; the whole executed in Stone. — The grand Front towards the Forest is adorned with a noble Portico of the *Corinthian* Order, and may with Propriety be considered as one of the finest Elevations in the Kingdom. It has, indeed, furnished Hints to succeeding Architects, but has perhaps never been rivalled by the many Imitations of it.*   The Garden Front is plainer, but is likewise in a good Style; in the Center is a Pediment, which contains a Bas Relief, supported by six three Quarter Columns.

The grand Hall is 53 Feet by 45; the Ornaments consist chiefly of two large antique Statues, *Livia* and *Domitian*, on Marble Pedestals, and three Pictures by *Casali*, viz. *Coriolanus*, *Porsenna*, and *Pompey* taking Leave of his Family. The Dining Room contains the following Paintings, also by the same Master: *Alexander* directing *Apelles* to paint *Campaspe*, the Continence of *Scipio*, and *Sophonisba* taking Poison. The Gallery or Ball Room is 75 Feet by 27, and is elegantly fitted up. The Saloon, and the Rest of the State Rooms are likewise decorated with Paintings, Sculpture, Tapestry, and other grand and suitable Ornaments.

The Park, though handsome and well planted, is not proportionably magnificent with the House; but as the Earl of *Tylney* is hereditary Ranger of *Epping Forest*, the whole of that extensive Tract may be considered as his Park. The grand Approach is through a long and beautiful Vista, which extends to the high Road at *Layton Stone*, and is terminated by a large Piece of Water, at a little Distance from the Front of the Building.

The Gardens are very large, adorned with ornamental Buildings, and finely watered, though in some Parts they partake of a greater Formality than is consistent with the present Taste.

* Among others, *Wentworth-House*, the Seat of the late Marquis of *Rockingham*, is nearly a direct Copy of *Wansted*.

Alnwick Castle, the Seat of the Duke of Northumberland.

Published as the Act directs Nov.r 1.st 1783 by W. Watts, Chelsea.

PLATE LVII.

ALNWICK CASTLE,

In NORTHUMBERLAND,

The Seat of his Grace the Duke of NORTHUMBERLAND.

(From a Drawing by the Right Honourable Lord Viscount DUNCANNON.)

ALNWICK CASTLE is fituated on the South Side of the River *Aln,* on an Elevation that gives great Dignity to its Appearance, and in ancient Times rendered it a moſt impregnable Fortreſs. From ſome *Roman* Mouldings found under the preſent Walks, it is ſuppoſed to have been founded in the Time of the *Romans,* although no Part of the original Structure is now remaining. — In the Reign of *William Rufus* it underwent a remarkable Siege from *Malcolm* III. King of *Scatland,* who loſt his Life before it, as did alſo Prince *Edward* his eldeſt Son ; and in the following Century *William* III. likewiſe King of *Scotland,* commonly called the *Lion,* was taken Priſoner beſieging this Caſtle. Before the *Norman* Conqueſt, it was in the Poſſeſſion of *Gilbert Tyſon,* a great Baron, who was ſlain with *Harold.* His Son *William* had an only Daughter, whom the Conqueror gave in Marriage to one of his *Norman* Chieftains, named *Ivo de Veſcy.* From that Period *Alnwick* Caſtle continued in the Poſſeſſion of the Lords *De Veſcy,* till the Time of *Edward* I. when it was granted to *Anthony Bec,* Biſhop of *Durham,* who in the Year 1309 ſold it to the Lord *Henry de Percy,* one of the greateſt Barons of the North, who immediately began to repair it, and afterwards, by his Succeſſors, both the Citadel and Out-works were compleated.

From Length of Time, and the Shocks it had ſuſtained in ancient Wars, it became nearly a Ruin, when, by the Death of *Algernon* Duke of *Somerſet* in 1750, it devolved with all the Eſtates to the preſent Duke and late Ducheſs, who immediately began the neceſſary Repairs, and with great Taſte and Judgment reſtored and embelliſhed it as much as poſſible in the Style it had originally been ; ſo that it may truly be conſidered as one of the nobleſt and moſt magnificent Models of a great baronial Caſtle.

It

It contains about five Acres of Ground within its Walls, which are flanked with fixteen Towers and Turrets, that now afford a complete Set of Offices to the Caftle, and retain, many of them, their original Names, as well as their ancient Ufe and Deftination. — The Caftle confifts of three Courts or Divifions, the Entrance to which was defended by as many ftrong maffy Gates, called the Utter Ward, the Middle Ward, and the Inner Ward. Each of thefe Gates was in a high embattled Tower, furnifhed with a Portcullis, and the outward one alfo with a Drawbridge. They had, each of them, a Porter's Lodge, and a ftrong Prifon; befides the neceffary Apartments for the Conftable, Bailiff, and fubordinate Officers. Under each of the Prifons was a deep and dark Dungeon, into which refractory Prifoners were let down with Cords, and from which there was no Exit but through the Trap-door in the Floor above. That of the inner Ward is ftill remaining in all its original Horror.

W. Beilby del.   W. Watts Sculp.

Keelder Castle *in Northumberland, the Seat of* **Earl Percy.**

Published as the Act directs Nov.r 1st 1783 by W. Watts, Chelsea

PLATE LVIII.

KEELDER CASTLE,

In *NORTHUMBERLAND*,

A Seat of the Right Honourable Earl P E R C Y.

(From a Drawing by Mr. WILLIAM BEILBY, of Battersea.)

KEELDER CASTLE is fituated in *Northumberland*, near the Borders of *Scotland*, between the River *Keelder* and the North *Tyne*, at their Confluence. It was built by Earl *Percy*, in the Style of a Caftle, (though fmall) and is chiefly ufed by his Lordfhip as a fhooting Seat.

The furrounding Country is very wild and uncultivated, and the Road to the Houfe, which is over Moors and Bogs, is for Horfemen only. From the Hills behind, which rife with uncommon Grandeur, the Profpect is very extenfive, commanding, in clear Weather, the Sea both to the Eaft and Weft.

H. Repton del.

W. Watts, Sculp.

Wolterton in Norfolk, the Seat of Lord Walpole.

Published as the Act directs Nov.r 1.st 1783 by W.Watts, Chelsea.

PLATE LIX.

W O L T E R T O N,

In N O R F O L K,

The Seat of the Right Honourable Lord W A L P O L E.

(From a Drawing by H U M P H R E Y R E P T O N, Efq.)

THIS Houfe was built, and the furrounding Plantations raifed, by the late Lord *Walpole*, of *Wolterton*, about Fifty-five Years fince. — A beautiful Piece of Water of about fourteen Acres forms a pleafing View from the South-Eaft Front of the Houfe, which likewife commands a diftant Profpect of the Woods and Park of the Earl of *Buckinghamfhire*, at *Blickling*. The Houfe is convenient, and well furnifhed.   It extends, in Front, an hundred Feet, and is feventy-five in Depth.

Carshalton House *in Surry, the Seat of* Theodore Henry Broadhead Esq.

Published as the Act directs Nov.r 3.rd 1783 by W. Watts, Chelsea.

W. Watts, del: et Sculp:

PLATE LX.

CARSHALTON HOUSE,

In SURRY,

The Seat of THEODORE HENRY BROADHEAD, Efq.

CARSHALTON HOUSE was built by the celebrated Doctor *Radcliffe*, who, from its healthy and pleafant Situation, ftyled it the *Montpelier* of *England*. It is a large and commodious Structure; the principal Room, which is the Library, is fixty-four Feet in Length.

The Grounds are laid out with great Tafte, and are finely watered by a remarkable clear Spring, the Head rifing at a little Diftance from the Houfe, which, after running through the Village of *Carfhalton*, falls into the River *Wandell*.

lord Duncannon, del:

W Watts, Sculp.

Ashburnham **Park** in Sussex, the Seat of the **Earl** of Ashburnham.

Publish'd as the Act directs June 1st 1784, by W Watts, Chelsea.

PLATE LXI.

ASHBURNHAM PARK,

In SUSSEX;

The Seat of the Right Honourable the Earl of ASBURNHAM.

(Drawn by the Right Honourable Lord Viscount DUNCANNON.)

ASHBURNHAM PARK is about Three Miles from *Battle*, Eight from *Haſtings*, and near Sixty from *London*. The Houſe is large, and pleaſantly ſituated in the Park, which is well wooded, and commands from the higher Ground a fine View of *Battle*, with the Bay of *Pevenſey* and *Beachy Head*. — The Pleaſure Grounds have been much improved by the preſent Earl, who has added ſeveral pleaſant Walks, with a large Piece of Water.

The Apartments contain ſome good Pictures by *Vandyke* and Sir *Peter Lely*, of the Family, which is of great Antiquity in this County. — *Aſhburnham*, (or, as it was then written *Eſhburnham)* was Sheriff of *Suſſex*, *Surry*, and *Kent*, and Conſtable of *Dover* Caſtle, in the Reign of King *Harold*; which Caſtle he defended againſt *William the Conqueror*, for which he was afterwards beheaded.

In the Church, which is behind the Houſe, they ſhew *Charles* I.'s Watch, Shirt, &c. which belonged to Colonel *Aſhburnham*, who was of his Bedchamber, and attended him at his Execution.

Robertson, del.   W. Watts, sculp.

Mount Clare *in Surry, the Seat of Sir John Dick Bar!*

Published as the Act directs June 4th 1784 by W. Watts, Chelsea.

PLATE LXII.

MOUNT - CLARE,

Near ROEHAMPTON, in SURRY;

A Villa belonging to Sir JOHN DICK, Baronet.

THIS House was built in the Year 1772, by the late *George Clive*, Esq. who, on Account of the happy Situation of the Ground, which commands a most pleasing View of *Richmond* Park, purchased it at the Rate of 300l. an Acre; and, in Compliment to the late Lord *Clive*, who was then Proprietor of *Clare-Mount*, called it *Mount-Clare*. — In the Year 1780 it became the Property of the present Owner; who has, with the Assistance of Signor *Placido Colombani*, a *Milanese* Architect, added a *Doric* Portico to it, and many architectural Ornaments, which renders it a compleat *Italian* Villa. Every Attention has also been paid in the Improvement of the Plantations and Grounds, which together form a *Ferme Ornée*.

Arno's Grove *in Middlesex, the Seat of* Isaac Walker Esq.

Published as the Act directs June 1st 1794 by W. Watts, Chelsea.

W. Watts, del. et sculp.

PLATE LXIII.

A R N O's G R O V E,

In M I D D L E S E X;

The Seat of ISAAC WALKER, Efq.

ARNO's GROVE is fituated at *Southgate*, a Village about ten Miles *North* of *London*. It was built by *James Colebrooke*, Efq. and, at his Death, became the Property of Sir *George Colebrooke*, Bart. who greatly improved and modernized the Grounds.

About the Year 1777 it was purchafed by the prefent Poffeffor, who has likewife made confiderable Improvements, and additional Walks in the Pleafure Grounds, which are now nearly Three Miles in Circuit. The *New River* winds for upwards of a Mile through the Valleys, and having been, by Permiffion of the *New-River Company*, increafed in Breadth, has a very pleafing Effect.

The Houfe was materially altered by Sir *George Colebrooke*, who built a Library and Eating Room in one of the Wings, under the Direction of Sir *Robert Tayler*, from Defigns nearly refembling the new Offices in the Bank of *England*. — The Library is 25 Feet by 20, and 20 in Heighth ; the Eating Room 35 Feet by 24, and 20 in Heighth.

The oppofite Wing was finifhed by Lord *Newhaven*, who had the Eftate a fhort Time before the prefent Owner. — It contains, likewife, an Eating Room, 25 Feet by 20, and 20 high. — A noble Hall, in the Center of the Houfe, leads to the Drawing Room, which is 36 Feet by 27. The Staircafe and Hall were painted by *Lanfcroon*.

The Situation of the Houfe is remarkably pleafant, commanding a View of feveral rich Valleys, with the Hills toward *Fincbley*, *Mufwell Hill*, &c.

High Legh in Cheshire, the Seat of Henry Cornwall Legh Esq.

Publish'd as the Act directs June 1st 1784 by W. Watts, Chelsea.

PLATE LXIV.

HIGH LEGH,

In CHESHIRE;

The Seat of HENRY CORNWALL LEGH, Esq.

(Painted by SAMUEL STRINGER, of Knutsford.)

THIS Edifice was rebuilt in the Reign of Queen *Elizabeth*, by *Thomas Legh*, Esq. from whom the prefent Poffeffor is lineally defcended: The Eftate on which it ftands was the Property of this very ancient and refpectable Family, at the time of the Conqueft. The Houfe is of Stone; the Front is efteemed elegant, in the Stile of Architecture of the Age it was built in.—It ftands in a pleafant Situation, on the Road between *Knutsford* and *Warrington*, and commands an extenfive Profpect over *Chefhire* and *Lancafhire*, bounded by the Wrekin in *Shropfhire*, and the Hills of *Staffordfhire*, *Derbyfhire*, and *Yorkfhire*. — The adjacent domeftic Chapel was erected by *Thomas Legh*, Esq. after he had completed the Houfe. His Family Arms, and the Date, 1581, yet remain on the outfide Wall: There were Paintings in the *Eaft* Window, well executed, which have been defaced by Time.

Collander, del.

W Watts, Sculp.

High Cliff in Hampshire, the Seat of the Earl of Bute.

Published as the Act directs Nov.r 1.st 1784 by W Watts, Chelsea.

PLATE LXV.

H I G H   C L I F F,

In *H A M P S H I R E*,

A Seat of the Right Honourable the Earl of B U T E.

(Drawn by —— C A L L A N D E R, from a Picture by Mr. S T E W A R T.)

T H E beautiful Situation of the small Common on which this Edifice stands induced the Proprietor to erect a little Box, which has been gradually enlarged as he acquired more Property about it. — The House fronts due South, directly opposite *Cherbourg*, distant sixty Miles.

The Needles of the *Isle of Wight* are, to the South-East, Eight Miles off, and *Hengerston Head* is in the South-West, forming the Bay of *Christ Church*, distant five Miles; which last View is here engraved, taking in the Town of *Christ Church*, and the Bay of *Pool*, seen over the Land.

J. Hilton, del.

W. Watts, Sculp.

The Seat of Sir John Elvill Bar.^t at Englefield Green in Surry.

Published as the Act directs Nov. 1.st 1784 by W. Watts, Chelsea.

PLATE LXVI.

The Seat of Sir JOHN ELVILL, Bart.

At ENGLEFIELD GREEN, in SURREY.

THIS elegant little Seat is fituated about two Miles beyond *Egham*, towards *Windfor* great Park, the Entrance to which is upon *Englefield Green*, and not far from the beautiful artificial Lake called the *Virginia* Water.

Englefield Green is about three Miles in Extent, and is embellifhed with a Number of delightful Manfions; its Vicinity to the Duke of *Cumberland*'s Lodge and *Windfor* Park and Foreft rendering it a moft defirable Situation.

W. Watts, del. et Sculp.

Godmerſham Park *in Kent, the Seat of* Thomas Knight Eſqr.

Publiſhed as the Act directs Nov.t 1ſt 1784, by W. Watts, Chelsea.

PLATE LXVII.

GODMERSHAM PARK,

In KENT,

The Seat of THOMAS KNIGHT, Esq.

GODMERSHAM PARK is about Eight Miles from *Canterbury*, and Fifty-seven from *London*. — The House is situated in a pleasant Valley, formed to the West by the Park, which has its Acclivity and Surfaces pleasingly broken and interspersed with different Clumps of Trees, and its Summit crowned with a very large Wood. — To the South it is terminated by a Sheep Down, which rises, in a bold Form, at a Quarter of a Mile from the House, and commands an extensive Prospect towards *Romney* and *Lid Castle*, and over the Weald of *Kent*, towards *Tunbridge Wells* and the *Suffex* Hills. — Along the Range of the Eastern and North-East Boundary, where the Ascent is at a greater Distance and more gradual, an agreeable Diversity of Outline is produced, and the contrasted Appearances of Agriculture and scattered Farm Houses enliven the Scene. — The River *Stour*, though not of a navigable Depth and Breadth, with a clear and no sluggish Current, winds its Course through the Village and fertile Meadows in the Bottom.

This Place was for many Years the Residence of the Family of *Birdnax*, who came into England with *William the Conqueror*, and from whom the present Owner is lineally descended. Their first Settlement was at *Saltwood Castle*, in this County, from whence they removed to *Godmersham*. — The Change of Name took Place upon a Devise of Property by Parliamentary Authority, in the Lifetime of the present Possessor's Father, who first laid out the Park and rebuilt the Mansion House.

Very considerable Alterations and Improvements have been lately made in the Approach to the House and Pleasure-Grounds contiguous.

W. Watts, del. et Sculp.

The Seat of Mrs. Garrick, at *Hampton* in Middlesex.

Published as the Act directs, Nov.1.st 1784, by W. Watts, Chelsea.

PLATE LXVIII.

The Seat of Mrs. G A R R I C K,

At HAMPTON, in MIDDLESEX.

THIS elegant Villa is fituated on the Banks of the *Thames*, about thirteen Miles Weft of *London*. — It was pur-chafed by the late Mr. *Garrick*, but had at that Time, excepting Situation, few Beauties to boaft of. Its Afpect was, however, in a fhort Time agreeably changed. The Building was new fronted, under the Direction of *Robert Adam*, Efq. and the Gardens were planted and modelled in their prefent beautiful Stile. The Houfe is handfomely furnifhed, and contains fome good Pictures, among which are fome Originals by *Hogarth*. — The Gardens and Pleafure-Grounds, though not above fix Acres in Extent, appear, from the judicious Arrangement and Diverfity, to be of much greater Magnitude. — At the North End is a Mount, which commands an extenfive View into *Surrey*; from whence, paffing, by gradual Defcent, through an Arch (over which is the high Road) a fine Profpect of the River, with *Moulfey Hurft*, prefents itfelf to View.

At the Weft End of the Terrace, and on the Margin of the River, is an elegant Temple, built by Mr. *Garrick*, and dedicated to *Shakefpeare*, whofe Statue, finely executed by *Roubilliac*, in white Marble, is placed within, on a Pedeftal fronting the Entrance.

Stewart pinx! & Callander delt.   W. Watts sculpt.

Luton in Bedfordshire the Seat of the Earl of Bute.

Published as the Act directs April 1st 1785 by W. Watts, Chelsea.

PLATE LXIX.

LUTON HOUSE,

In BEDFORDSHIRE.

The Seat of the Right Honourable the Earl of BUTE.

(Drawn by —— CALLANDER, from a Picture by Mr. STEWART.)

THIS House was built by the present Earl of *Bute*, near a very antient Dwelling, formerly the Residence of the Family of *Hoo*, and in later Days, of the *Napiers*. It is situated on a gently rising Ground, in a large Park finely wooded. The River *Lee*, which runs through it, has, on its Entrance into the Park, been widened to several hundred Feet.

W. Watts, del: et Sculp.

Osterly Park in Middlesex, the Seat of Mrs Child.

Published as the Act directs April 1st 1785 by W. Watts, Chelsea.

PLATE LXX.

OSTERLEY HOUSE,

In *MIDDLESEX*,

The Seat of Mrs. CHILD,

IS fituated near the Center of a beautiful Park, about ten Miles North Weft of *London*. The Site of the prefent Structure, and Part of the Demefne appurtenant to it, were formerly Parcel of the Domains of the Convent at *Sion*, which had been founded by *Henry* V. for Nuns of the Order of St. *Bridget*. After the Diffolution of that Monaftery, this Eftate, among others, was granted by the Crown to the Protector, Duke of *Somerfet*; upon whofe Attainder it reverted, and was granted, with the Manor of *Hefton*, by Queen *Elizabeth*, in the Twelfth Year of her Reign, to Sir *Thomas Grefham*, (as appears by the Letters Patent, now remaining in the Chapel of the Rolls) who erected the Manfion which is the Subject of this Defcription.

From Sir *Thomas Grefham* it paffed to other Owners, till the beginning of the prefent Century; when it became the Property of Sir *Robert Child*, from whom it has defcended, by regular Succeffion, to *Robert Child*, Efq. the laft male Survivor of that ancient and very refpectable Family; who, in the Courfe of the preceding Fifteen Years, rebuilt the Shell, ornamented, beautified, and new furnifhed the whole, in a Style of Elegance and Magnificence, that evince at once both his Tafte and Liberality.

The Houfe is large, and of a quadrangular Form : It extends from Eaft to Weft 140 Feet, and from North to South 117, and has a Turret at each Angle. The principal Front is decorated with a Portico, of the Ionic Order, from whence a fpacious Court leads to the Saloon, an elegant Apartment, alfo of the Ionic Order, 44 Feet by 33, fuperbly ornamented and enriched with antique Marble Statues, Baffo Relievos, Vafes, &c. Oppofite the grand Entrance of the Saloon, a Corridor leads to the

Picture

Picture Gallery, which is 130 Feet in length by 22, and contains a choice Collection of Pictures by the beſt Maſters. From the North and South Ends of the Gallery, Corridors lead to Suites of private and ſtate Apartments; the former conſiſting of a Dining Room, Library, and Breakfaſt Parlour; and the latter, which extends from Eaſt to Weſt, the whole Length of the South Front, of a magnificent Drawing Room, State Bed Rooms, &c. Theſe Apartments are decorated in the moſt ſplendid Manner, with Hangings of Silk, Damaſk, Velvet, and Gobelin Tapeſtry; Paintings, Marble Chimney Pieces, Carvings, enrich'd Entablatures, Moſaic Work, &c. &c.

The Gardens and Park have alſo, within the Period above mentioned, been modernized and improved. The adjacent Country being rather flat, the Views are few; but thoſe from the principal Front, towards *Highgate* and *Hampſtead*, from the North to *Harrow*, and the South to *Richmond* and other Hills in *Surrey*, are very picturesque and romantic, and receive additional Beauty from two fine Sheets of Water, which run in an oblique Direction near the South and Eaſt Fronts of the Houſe.

Lord Duncannon, del.   *W. Watts, Sculp.*

Lulworth Castle *in Dorsetshire, the Seat of* Humphry Weld Esq.

Publish'd as the Act directs April 1.st 1788 by W. Watts, Chelsea.

PLATE LXXI.

LULWORTH CASTLE,

In *DORSETSHIRE*,

The Seat of HUMPHREY WELD, Efquire.

(From a Drawing by the Right Honourable Lord Vifcount DUNCANNON.)

LULWORTH Caftle is fituated on the Coaft of *Dorfetfhire*, near *Wareham*, on a rifing Ground, and commands a delightful Profpect of the Sea, from an Opening between two Hills, which protect it from the violent Winds.

The Caftle is an exact Cube of eighty Feet, with a round Tower at each Corner thirty Feet in Diameter, rifing fixteen Feet above the Walls of the Building, which are fix Feet thick, and are, as well as the Towers, embattled. The Offices are under Ground, and are arched with Stone.

There appears from *Tyrrel*'s Hiftory of *England*, to have been a Caftle here as early as the Year 1146, when " *Robert* " Earl of *Gloucefter* took the Caftle of *Lullwarde* for the Emprefs *Maud*." The prefent Edifice was, however, erected in the Year 1609, by *Thomas Howard*, Vifcount *Bindon*, and was purchafed, in 1641, by *Humphrey Weld*, Efquire; in whofe Family it has continued ever fince.

The prefent Poffeffor has new fitted up the Apartments, many of which are large, very elegantly. The Dining Room is fifty feet by twenty five, and eighteen in Height.

At this Seat King *James* I. was entertained in the Year 1615; as was alfo King *Charles* II. with the Dukes of *York* and *Monmouth*, in 1665. It is likewife celebrated for having been garrifoned by *Charles* I., and afterwards by the Parliament Forces; who, upon breaking up the Garrifon, fold or demolifhed great Quantities of Wainfcoting, Iron, Lead, and other Materials of this noble Pile.

The Grounds are beautifully laid out, and are ornamented with fine Wood, which is, in general, very fcarce on this Coaft.

The View annexed was taken from a Summer Houfe in the Garden in the Year 1784.

Chilham Castle *in Kent the Seat of* Tho.? Heron Esq.?

Published as the Act directs April 1st 1785. by W. Watts, Chelsea.

W. Watts, del. et sc.

PLATE LXXII.

The South-West View of CHILHAM CASTLE,

In KENT,

The Seat of THOMAS HERON, Esquire.

CHILHAM Castle stands in a pleasant Park, about six Miles South West from *Canterbury*, on the Road to *Ashford*. It is a spacious, stately Mansion, finely situated for the Command of several beautiful Prospects, particularly of a Valley below it, which is watered by the River *Stour*. It was built in the Beginning of the last Century by Sir *Dudley Digges*, on the Site of the ancient Castle, which is supposed to have been erected by *Fulbert de Dover*; of which the Keep (formerly of great Strength) still remains; and being covered with remarkably fine Ivy, makes a most venerable and romantic Appearance.

From the Vessels taken up here, on digging the Foundations of the present Mansion, there is no Doubt of *Chilham* having been a *Roman* Station; and *Cæsar* is said to have encamped here, on his second Expedition into *Britain*. In the Time of the *Saxon* Heptarchy, it was the Residence of the Kings of *Kent*; but was afterwards sacked and demolished by the *Danes*. *Sired*, a *Saxon*, who had great Possessions in *Kent*, held *Chilham* of *Edward the Confessor*; he was in the Battle of *Hastings*, on the Side of *Harold*, and was therefore dispossessed by *William the Conqueror*, who granted it to *Fulbert de Dover*. Anciently, as was customary in various other Honours and Baronies, *this* was sometimes called by the Name of the Owner; from whence it came to be stiled *The Barony of Fobert*. In the fifteenth Year of King *John*, (being in the Crown) that King granted the Custody of the Castle of *Chilham*, with the Honour and its Appurtenances, to *Thomas Peverel*. Nineteen Manors in *Kent* were held of it by Knights Service; and great Privileges and Immunities, with several extensive Denberries in the Weald of *Kent*, were annexed to it.

After

After the Family of *Fulbert de Dover*, (whofe Defcendants affumed the Name of *Lucy,)* it was fuccefively held, except when in the Crown, by Forfeiture, or other Incident of the feodal Tenures, by *Richard le Fitz Roy*, Son of *John* King of *England*; and *Alexander Baliol*, Brother to *John* King of *Scotland*, in right of their Wives, who were Heirs to *Fulbert de Dover*; by the *Strathbolgies*, Earls of *Athol*, in *Scotland*; the Lords *Badlefmere* and *Roos*; Sir *John Scott*, of *Scottfhall*; *Thomas* Earl of *Rutland*; and the Families of *Cheney*, *Kempe*, *Digges*, and *Colebrooke*. It was held in Capite, by the Service of Caftle-Guard at *Dover* Caftle. *Alexander de Baliol*, and *David de Strathbolgy*, Earl of *Athol*, (although Subjects of *Scotland)* were fummoned to Parliament, and on military Services, amongft the *Englifh* Barons, as being poffeffed of the Honour of *Chilham*.

The late *Robert Colebrooke*, Efquire, alienated *Chilham*, in the Year 1774, (under the Authority of an Act of Parliament,) to *Thomas Heron*, of *Newark*, in the County of *Nottingham*, Efquire, Heir male of the Family of the *Herons*, of *Bokenfield*, in *Northumberland*, who hath much improved this ancient Seat.

Stewart. Pinx.? Callander. del.?   W. Watts. Sculp.?

Mount-stuart House in the *Isle of Bute, the Seat of the* Earl of Bute.

Published as the Act directs Sep.t 1785, by W. Watts, Chelsea.

PLATE LXXIII.

MOUNTSTUART HOUSE,

In the Isle of BUTE.

The Seat of the Right Honourable the Earl of BUTE.

(Drawn by —— CALLANDER, from a Picture by Mr. STEWART.)

THIS House, which was built by the late Earl of *Bute* in the Year 1718, is situated on the East Coast of the Island of *Bute*, within half a Mile of the Sea.—It was not entirely finished at his Death.

The Gardens and Pleasure Grounds, which are very extensive, were likewise laid out by his Lordship—Being built on the Side of a Hill, it commands a fine Prospect of the Sea and neighbouring Country,

Penny, del.

W. Watts, sculp.

Castle Hill in Devonshire, the Seat of Lord Fortescue.

Publish'd as the Act directs Sep.r 1.st 1785, by W. Watts, Chelsea.

PLATE LXXIV.

C A S T L E   H I L L,

In DEVONSHIRE.

The Seat of the Right Honourable Lord FORTESCUE.

(From a Drawing by Mr. FEARY.)

CASTLE HILL is fituated in the North of *Devonfhire*, about eight Miles from *Barnftaple*.

The Houfe and Grounds were materially altered and modernized by the late Earl *Clinton*, and have fince received additional Improvements by the late Lord *Fortefcue*.

The Grounds are of confiderable Extent, and afford a beautiful Diverfity of Wood, Water, and Lawn.

G. Hearne del.

W. Watts, sculp.

Prior Park *in Somersetshire, the Seat of* M.rs Smith.

Publish'd as the Act directs Sep.r 1.st 1785, by W. Watts, Chelsea.

PLATE LXXV.

PRIOR PARK,

In SOMERSETSHIRE.

The Seat of Mrs. SMITH.

(Drawn by T. HEARNE.)

THIS elegant Manſion is ſituated near the ſummit of *Charlton* Hill, in the Neighbourhood of *Bath*, and commands, from the principal Front, fine Proſpects of that City and its Environs.

It was built by the late celebrated *Ralph Allen*, Eſquire, and conſiſts of a Center and wings united by Arcades, forming one line of Building, one thouſand Feet in extent. The whole Fabric is of Stone, and is of the *Corinthian* Order. The Apartments are ſpacious, and finiſhed in a magnificent Taſte.

The Gardens are laid out with Elegance, and (being on the Declivity of the Hill) receive additional Beauties from the Inequality of Ground. The Walks, which ſerpentine through this delightful Spot, are decorated with Vaſes, and other Ornaments in Stone, and are refreſhed by an ample Supply of Water, which is diſperſed in ſmall Streams, and Water Falls with great Taſte and Propriety.

J. Chubbard. Pinxt.

W. Watts. Sculpt.

Woolton Hall in Lancashire, the Seat of Nicholas Ashton Esqr.

Published as the Act directs Sep. 1, 1785, by W. Watts, Chelsea.

PLATE LXXVI.

WOOLTON HALL,

In LANCASHIRE.

The Seat of NICHOLAS ASHTON, Esquire.

(From a Picture by Mr. CHUBBARD, of Liverpool.)

WOOLTON HALL is situated about six Miles from Liverpool, upon an Eminence, and commands grand and extensive Prospects, the two extreme Points of View being the Cumberland and Westmoreland Hills to the North, and the Wreakin near Shrewsbury to the South; from hence may also be distinctly seen Blackstone Edge in Yorkshire and several of the Derbyshire and Staffordshire Hills; to the Eastward the Rivers Mersey and Weaver join in View, about four Miles, from the House, and very soon opening into a fine Sheet of Water, continue their Course to the Port of Liverpool. The Prospect to the South West is terminated by an irregular Line of Welsh Mountains.

W. Beilby. del.

W. Watts. Sculp.

Axwell Park *in the County of Durham, the Seat of* Sir Tho.ˢ Clavering Bar.ᵗ

Publish'd as the Act directs Jany 1.ˢᵗ 1786, by W. Watts, Chelsea.

PLATE LXXVII.

AXWELL PARK,

In the County of DURHAM,

The Seat of Sir THOMAS CLAVERING, Baronet.

(From a Drawing by Mr. BEILBY, of BATTERSEA.*)*

AXWELL PARK is fituated on a Point of Land between the Rivers *Tyne* and *Derwent*, having the Junction of thofe Rivers, and the Town of *Newcaftle* to the Eaft, in full view. The Houfe ftands on the South-eaft Declivity of a beautiful Hill, finely wooded, which effectually fhelters it from the North and North Weft. The Afcent is eafy, through a fmall Wood, which opens into a Lawn, and affords agreeable Views. To the South and South Weft the Profpect extends over the Tops of the Woods to the neighbouring Country, particularly on the oppofite Side of the *Derwent*, where the Ground rifes, by gentle Afcents, for feveral Miles.

This Edifice was raifed by the prefent Baronet on the Site of the ancient Family Manfion called *White Houfe*, in the Year 1758, under the Direction of *James Paine*, Efquire.

W.Watts, del. et Sculp.

Olantigh in Kent, the Seat of **John Sawbridge Esq.**

Publish'd as the Act directs Jan.y 1st 1786, by W.Watts, Chelsea.

PLATE LXXVIII.

OLANTIGH,

In *KENT*,

The Seat of JOHN SAWBRIDGE, Esquire.

OLANTIGH is situated in a pleasant Part of the County of *Kent*, about two Miles from *Godmersham* and ten from *Canterbury*. The original Structure on this Spot appears to have been an Oratory or Chapel, erected by Cardinal *Kemp*. The Mansion was built by Sir *Thomas Kemp*, who was created Knight of the Bath at the Marriage of Prince *Arthur*, eldest Son to King *Henry* VII. His Descendant (also Sir *Thomas Kemp)* having no male Issue, left the Estate to his four Daughters, who joined in a Sale of it to Sir *Timothy Thornhill*; from whose Family it was purchased, in the Year 1717, by *Jacob Sawbridge*, Esquire, Grandfather to *John Sawbridge*, Esquire, the present Possessor, who has greatly improved the Place.

Near the House is a very considerable Mount, called *Barrow Hill*, which is upwards of one hundred Feet in Height, and more than half a Mile in Circumference at the Base: From its Name it has been considered as a *Tumulus*; but this Conjecture appears to be ill founded.

C. Vatou. del.

W. Watts, Sculp.

Lyme Hall in *Cheshire, the Seat of* **Peter Legh** Esqr.

Publish'd as the Act directs Jany 1st 1786 by W. Watts, Chelsea.

PLATE LXXIX.

LYME HALL,

In *CHESHIRE*,

The Seat of PETER LEGH, Efquire.

(From a Drawing by CLAUDE NATES.)

LYME HALL, the Seat of the ancient and refpectable Family of the *Leghs*, is fituated in a fmall, but pleafant, Park, in the Hundred of *Macclesfield*, in the North-eaft Part of the County Palatine of *Chefter*, diftant from *Stockport* about fix Miles, and near the Road leading from that Town to *Derby*. The Houfe is large and commodious, and commands fine Views of the neighbouring Country.

In the Oratory belonging to the *Leghs* of *Lyme* (on the South Side of the parochial Chapel at *Macclesfield)* there is an ancient Epitaph on *Perkin a Legh*, the Anceftor of this Family, who received the Lordfhip of *Lyme* from King *Edward* III., as a Reward for taking the Count of *Tankerville* Prifoner, and other military Services in *France*, particularly at the Battle of *Creffy*. There is alfo an Epitaph on Sir *Piers Legh*, his Son, who was killed at the memorable Battle of *Agincourt*. Thefe Infcriptions were found on a Stone in the Chapel in the Year 1626, by Sir *Peter Legh*, and, by his Direction, were at that Time engraved on a Brafs Plate.

C. Nixon. del   W. Watts Sculp.

Broughton Tower in Lancashire, the Seat of John Gilpin Sawrey Esq.

Publish'd as the Act directs Jan.y 1st 1786 by W. Watts, Chelsea.

PLATE LXXX.

BROUGHTON TOWER,

In *LANCASHIRE*,

The Seat of JOHN GILPIN SAWREY, Esquire,

(From a Drawing by CLAUDE NATES.)

BROUGHTON TOWER is situated in that Part of *Lancashire* called *Furness*, upon an Eminence commanding an extensive Prospect down the River *Duddon*, (which divides the Counties of *Lancaster* and *Cumberland*,) and also a distant View of the *Irish* Sea. *Blackcomb*, a high Mountain in *Cumberland*, intercepts the Prospect of the *Isle of Man*, which may be distinctly seen from the rising Grounds above the House when the Atmosphere is clear; also the *Isle of Anglesey* and the *Welch* Mountains, at the Distance of more than one hundred Miles.

The Tower is, in a great Measure, hid by the modern House, which encloses it on three Sides; but the North-east Front remains in its antient Form, considerably elevated above the new Building, from whence there is a most romantic View of near and distant Mountains, terminated by *Hard-knot* Hill, in *Cumberland*.

The Grounds adjoining are laid out in a Style suitable to the Situation of the House; and the neighbouring Hills are planted with *Scots* Fir.

This is a Place of great Antiquity, being the chief Seat of the *Broughtons* in the Time of the *Anglo-Saxons*. Sir *Thomas Broughton*, in the Reign of *Henry* VII. was the last Possessor of that Name. He was killed at the Battle of *Stokefield*, in the Year 1478; upon which *Henry* VII. granted the Manor to the Earls of *Derby*, and they, in the Reign of *James* I. to the *Leighs*, who sold it to the Ancestors of the present Possessor.

P. Sandby R.A. del.

W. Watts, sculp.

Chatsworth in *Derbyshire*, the Seat of the Duke of Devonshire.

Published as the Act directs May 20.th 1786, by W. Watts, Chelsea.

PLATE LXXXI.

CHATSWORTH,

In *DERBYSHIRE*,

The Seat of His Grace the Duke of DEVONSHIRE.

(Drawn by PAUL SANDBY, Esquire, R. A.)

THE Manfion Houfe at *Chatfworth* was begun by Sir *William Cavendifh*, in the Reign of Queen *Elizabeth*, and finifhed after his Death by his Lady in fo magnificent a Style, that it was at that Time ranked among the Wonders of the *Peak*. It has fince that Period been much enlarged and improved, and at prefent may undoubtedly vie, in point of Grandeur, with the firft Places in this Kingdom. The whole Building is of an excellent Stone, veined like Marble, which has been hewn from the neighbouring Quarries : It confifts of four regular Fronts, of different Architecture, with an inner Court, adorned with a Piazza of the *Doric* Order. The Houfe ftands about fix Miles S. W. of *Chefterfield*, having the River *Derwent* to the Weft, and a prodigious Acclivity to the Eaft, finely planted to its Summit with Firs. From the Top of this Afcent a vaft Plain extends itfelf near fourteen Miles to the North, containing a Refervoir, or Piece of Water, of about thirty Acres, which amply fupplies the Gardens, Fountains, Cafcades, &c. The Garden Front has the Motto of the Family, " CAVENDO TVTVS," extending the whole Length of the Frize. From this Part of the Building there is a fine Profpect over the Gardens towards *Hardwicke*, another Seat of the Duke's, which has been attained by removing a confiderable Mountain that intercepted the View.

 This Place is remarkable for having been the Prifon (if fuch a Place can be fo called) of *Mary* the unfortunate Queen of *Scots*, as well as of Marefchal *Tallard*, who was taken Prifoner at the Battle of *Blenheim*.

 Great Alterations were made here by the late Mr. *Brown*, who modernized the Park and Grounds, improved the Water, erected an handfome Bridge, and deftroyed the general Formalities of the Place. The Waterworks, indeed, yet exift, but they are confidered only as mere Matters of Curiofity and Expence, and the Remains of that Species of Garden Magnificence which has long been exploded by a happy Attention to the Power and Beauties of Nature.

R. Wilson pinx.ᵗ   W.ᵗ Watts, Sculp.

Wilton *in* *Wiltshire*, *the Seat of the* **Earl** *of* **Pembroke**.

Published as the Act directs May 20th 1786, by W.ᵗ Watts, Chelsea.

PLATE LXXXII.

WILTON HOUSE,

In WILTSHIRE,

The Seat of the Right Honourable the Earl of PEMBROKE.

(From a Picture by R. WILSON, in the Possession of PAUL PANTON, Esquire, of Lincoln's Inn.)

THIS celebrated Edifice is situated in a pleasant Vale about three Miles from *Salisbury*. It was begun in the Reign of *Henry* VIII. on the Ruins of a sequestered Abbey, and was afterwards enlarged at different Times by its various Possessors, particularly about the Year 1640, when *Philip* Earl of *Pembroke* rebuilt a considerable Part, from the Designs of *Inigo Jones*. The Gardens are on the South Side of the House, and are watered by the River *Willy*, over which is the admired Palladian Bridge, built by the late Earl, and esteemed one of the most beautiful of the Kind in *England*.

As it is not possible to describe the many valuable Antiquities, Paintings, &c. at this Place, within the Limits of this Work, a few of the most remarkable only will be pointed out. In the Court before the House is a Column of *Egyptian* Marble, the Shaft of which is near seventy Hundred Weight, and is of one Piece; it was brought from *Rome*, and is now crowned with a Statue of *Venus*; there is also on each Side of the Entrance, a Statue of black Marble brought from *Egypt*. In the great Gateway is a Statue of *Shakespeare*, by *Scheemaker*, with the Lines from *Macbeth*, " Life's but a " walking Shadow," &c. The Porch, which was built by *Hans Holbein*, contains Busts of *Hannibal*, *Miltiades*, &c. The Vestibule is ornamented with a fine Statue of *Apollo*, some antique Busts, and two Columns of *Paionet*, or Peacock Marble, each nine Feet seven Inches in Height. In the great Hall is a Statue of *Faustina*, and at the Foot of the Stair-case is a *Bacchus*, as large as Life, executed in *Peloponnesian* Marble. Among the Pictures are, the admired Family Piece, by *Vandyke*, twenty Feet by twelve; the Assumption of the Virgin, by *Raphael*; John the Baptist, by *Palma*; Christ washing St. Peter's Feet, by *Tintoret*; a capital Piece, by *Rubens*, of four Children; a Nativity, by the same Master; a Fruit Piece, by *Michael Angelo*; the Decollation of St. John, by *Dobson*; with a curious Painting of *Richard* II. in his Youth, praying to the Virgin Mary, executed about the Year 1377, of which there is an Engraving by *Hollar*.

It was at this Place that Sir *Philip Sidney* wrote his *Arcadia*; from which Romance several Incidents are delineated on the Pannels of the Saloon.

W. Tomkins pinxt.

W. Watts, sculp.

Bryanston in Dorsetshire, the Seat of Heny. Wm. Portman Esqr.

Published as the Act directs May 20th 1786, by W. Watts, Chelsea.

PLATE LXXXIII.

B R Y A N S T O N,

In DORSETSHIRE,

The Seat of HENRY-WILLIAM-BERKELEY PORTMAN, Esquire.

(From a Picture by WILLIAM TOMKINS, Esquire.)

BRYANSTON, according to the earliest Accounts now extant, was formerly in the Possession of *Bryan de Insula*, one of the great feudal Barons in the Reign of King *John*. It afterwards passed into other Families, and was, in the Reign of *Charles* the First, purchased by Sir *William Portman*, of *Orchard Portman*, Baronet, whose Descendant, in the Year 1695, devised it to *Henry Seymour*, Esquire, fifth Son of Sir *Edward Seymour*, of *Bury Pomeroy*, in the County of *Devon*, Baronet, with Remainder, in Default of Issue, to *William Berkeley*, of *Pylle*, in the County of *Somerset*, Esquire, a younger Branch of the Family of the Lord *Berkeley* of *Stratton*, and descended from the ancient Barons of *Berkeley Castle*.

It is now in the Possession of his Grandson, *Henry-William-Berkeley Portman*, Esquire, from whom it has received great Improvements, the House being entirely new built of Freestone, from the Designs of *James Wyatt*, Esquire, nearly on the Site of the ancient Mansion; its Dimensions are 112 Feet by 100, the Offices are contained in a separate Building on the West Side of the House, and are very spacious and convenient, communicating with the House by an enclosed Passage. The Hall, which is to the East, is 24 Feet by 30, and has a large Nich facing the Door of Entrance, eight Feet deep, which leads to an octangular Staircase, 30 Feet diameter, in the Center of the House, with a Gallery round, level with the Bedchamber Story, and communicating to all the Apartments on that Floor. This Gallery is formed by eight Scagliola Columns and eight Pilasters, and have, together with the other well-chosen Ornaments, a most beautiful Effect. To the Right of the Hall, as you enter, is an Eating Room, 24 Feet by 36, and 18 high; and to the Left, a Drawing Room, of the same Dimensions; beyond the Drawing Room, facing the South, is a Music Room, 25 Feet by 40; and at the End of that, facing the South likewise, is a Library, 24 Feet by 30, and of the same Height as those before mentioned. These Apartments are finished in a most elegant Style, and are justly admired for their agreeable Proportions, as well as for the Beauty and Grandeur of their Decorations.

The House stands on an extensive Lawn, skirted with a beautiful hanging Wood, a Mile and a half in length, with the River *Stour* winding through the Center of the Lawn, which, with the View of the Bridge and Town of *Blandford*, and of the Downs of *Dorsetshire*, interspersed with Woods, form a most delightful and pleasing Prospect.

T. Malton, del.

W. Watts, sculp.

Heath in Yorkshire, the Seat of John Smyth Esqr.

Published as the Act directs May 20th 1786, by W. Watts, Chelsea.

PLATE LXXXIV.

H E A T H,

In YORKSHIRE,

The Seat of JOHN SMYTH, Efquire,

(From a Drawing by THOMAS MALTON, junior.)

HEATH, the Seat of *John Smyth*, Efquire, is fituated in a pleafant Village of the fame Name, about a Mile from the Town of *Wakefield* in *Yorkfhire*. It was erected about thirty Years fince, by the late *John Smyth*, Efquire, from the Defigns of Mr. *Carr*, of *York*, and though not exactly conformable to the prefent Tafte, may with Propriety be confidered as an elegant Compofition in Architecture. It commands, from the Front, extenfive Views of a fine Country, diverfified by the River *Calder* and the Town of *Wakefield*,

THE ENGLISH LANDSCAPE GARDEN

1   Dydymus Mountain (i.e., Thomas Hill). *The Gardeners Labyrinth*. London, 1594.

2   Gervase Markham. *The English Husbandman* (Books I and II). London, 1613 and 1614.

3   William Lawson. *A New Orchard and Garden*. London, 1618.
      bound with
John Marriott. *Knots for Gardens*. London, 1625.
      bound with
Ralph Austen. *A Treatise of Fruit-trees* together with *The Spirituall use of an Orchard*. Oxford, 1653.

4   Isaac de Caus. *Wilton Garden*. London, c. 1645.
      bound with
_____. *New and Rare Inventions of Water-Works*. London, 1659.

5   John Worlidge. *Systema Horti-culturae: or, The Art of Gardening*. London, 1677.

6   Jean de la Quintinie (trans. John Evelyn). *The Compleat Gard'ner*. London, 1693.

7   Timothy Nourse. *Campania Foelix*. London, 1700.

8 François Gentil (trans. George London and Henry Wise). *The Retir'd Gard'ner.* London, 1706. Two volumes.

9 John Laurence. *Gardening Improv'd.* London, 1718.

10 Stephen Switzer. *Ichnographia Rustica: or, The Nobleman, Gentleman, and Gardener's Recreation.* London, 1718. Three volumes.

11 Batty Langley. *New Principles of Gardening.* London, 1728.

12 Robert Castell. *The Villas of the Ancients Illustrated.* London, 1728.

13 Stephen Switzer. *An Introduction to a General System of Hydrostaticks and Hydraulicks, Philosophical and Practical.* London, 1729. Two volumes:

14 Robert Morris. *An Essay upon Harmony As it relates chiefly to Situation and Building.* London, 1739.
     bound with
   John Trusler. *Elements of Modern Gardening.* London, 1784.

15 John Serle. *A Plan of Mr. Pope's Garden.* London, 1745.
     bound with
   Gardens at Richmond, Kew, and Environs. London, ?1730–1760.

16 *The Gardens at Stowe.* London, 1732—1797.

17 Jean Denis Attiret (trans. Joseph Spence). *A Particular Account of the Emperor of China's Gardens Near Pekin.* London, 1752.
     bound with
   William Shenstone. *Unconnected Thoughts on Gardening* and *A Description of the Leasowes.* London, 1764.
     bound with
   George Mason. *An Essay on Design in Gardening.* London, 1768.

18 Horace Walpole. *The History of the Modern Taste in Gardening.* London, 1827.
     bound with
   _____. *Journals of Visits to Country Seats.* Oxford, 1928.

19 Thomas Whately. *Observations on Modern Gardening.* London, 1770.

20 Joseph Heely. *Letters on the Beauties of Hagley, Envil, and the Leasowes.* London, 1777.

21 William Watts. *The Seats of the Nobility and Gentry In a Collection of the most interesting and Picturesque Views.* London, 1779.

22 William Mason. *The English Garden.* London, 1783.

23 René Louis de Girardin (trans. Daniel Malthus). *An Essay on Landscape.* London, 1783.
   bound with
A Tour to Ermenonville. London, 1785.

24 William Angus. *The Seats of the Nobility and Gentry in Great Britain and Wales.* London, 1787.

25 William Mavor. *New Description of Blenheim.* London, 1793.

26 Humphry Repton. *Fragments on the Theory and Practice of Landscape Gardening.* London, 1816.

27 George W. Johnson. *A History of English Gardening, Chronological, Biographical, Literary, and Critical.* London, 1829.

28 J. C. Loudon. *An Encyclopaedia of Gardening.* London, 1835. Two volumes.

29 _____. *The Suburban Gardener, and Villa Companion.* London, 1838.